TIMOTHY GREEN BECKLEY'S

UFO SPIN DOCTORS

PROOF ALIENS CAN BE DETRIMENTAL TO YOUR WELL BEING

Around and around the saucers go, where they will land nobody knows.

Timothy Green Beckley's UFO Spin Doctors
FULL COLOR EDITION

By Sean Casteel and Timothy Green Beckley

Copyright © 2020

By Timothy Green Beckley dba Inner Light/Global Communications

All Rights Reserved

No part of these manuscripts may be copied or reproduced by any mechanical or digital methods and no excerpts or quotes may be used in any other book or manuscript without permission in writing by the Publisher, Inner Light/Global Communications, except by a reviewer who may quote brief passages in a review.

Timothy Green Beckley: Editorial Director
Carol Rodriguez: Publishers Assistant
Editor and Layout: Tim R. Swartz
Sean Casteel: Associate Editor
William Kern: Editorial Assistant

Published in the United States of America
By Inner Light/Global Communications
Box 753, New Brunswick, NJ 08903

www.ConspiracyJournal.com

Email: MrUFO8@hotmail.com

CONTENTS

SPIN, SPIN, SPIN – AS THE FLYING SAUCERS TURN 7

CHAPTER 1 - A Classic Case of the Men In Black 23

CHAPTER 2 - The Top Secret Treaty Between the U.S. and Aliens 23

CHAPTER 3 - David Bowie – "Starman" 37

CHAPTER 4 - The Mass Landing Myth and The Armies of God 47

CHAPTER 5 – UFOs and Prophecies of the Presidents 55

CHAPTER 6 - Contacting Aliens and Angels With Sacred Symbols 65

CHAPTER 7 - "Pale Prophet" or Ancient Alien? 73

CHAPTER 8 - Haunted Treasure and Connection with UFOs 81

CHAPTER 9 - The Murderous Mystery of the Bell Witch 91

CHAPTER 10 - The Dog-Awful Truth Behind "Cryptid Creatures" 97

CHAPTER 11 - UFOS, Mediumship and the Paranormal 111

CHAPTER 12 - Was Inventor Nikola Tesla a UFO Contactee? 123

CHAPTER 13 - Diane Tessman - UFO Investigator/Cosmic Citizen 131

UFO SPIN DOCTORS

Above: A long haired Tim Beckley talks movies with Robert Wise, director of "The Day The Earth Stood Still."

Below: A fledgling rock star, Beckley dazzles fans while drummer Bleu Ocean picks up the beat.

SPIN, SPIN, SPIN – AS THE FLYING SAUCERS TURN
By Timothy Green Beckley

We are at the mercy of the Spin Doctors.

Originally the term "Spin Doctor" refereed to a political press agent or publicist employed to promote a favorable interpretation of events. That is, events which probably did not happen precisely as described, but which could be altered to rise to the occasion. If you can put the right amount of spin on a situation you can make someone, or an entire group, believe almost anything. Even if it never happened that way.

The worst case scenario—a terrible nightmare – can become your best asset if you can rectify the events and place them in a favorable light. Look at the O.J. Simpson trial.

"One on line source explains further that the word is, "Often associated with newspapers and politicians, to use spin is to manipulate meaning, to twist truth for particular ends--usually with the aim of persuading readers or listeners that things are other than they are. As in idioms such as to put a 'positive spin on something'—or a 'negative spin on something'—one line of meaning is concealed, while another—at least intentionally—takes its place. Spin is language which, for whatever reason, has designs on us…"

In the world of UFOlogy there is plenty of spit. No matter how hard core the evidence for a particular case may be, your hard noses skeptic will say that there is a "logical explanation," that that craft that crashed in the woods was actually just a meteor (even if it shot back up into the sky).

UFO SPIN DOCTORS

Likewise, a case that is of little merit can be bolstered over and over through talk shows and podcasts, until a story has been cemented in "fact."

We have put the best spin possible on the events described in the text of this book. The incidents in quest all have great merit, more so in the way they are told. Furthermore, to justify the "Doctor" in the title we have dug into our files to find a startling report on the Men in Black as described by the late Dr. Berthold Eric Swartz.

You are welcome to hop on board and spin around and around with us and our Ultra-Terrestrial friends.

And who knows what side of the galaxy we might end up in!

The Men In Black have long been associated with close encounters and other bizarre paranormal phenomena.

CHAPTER 1

A Classic Case of the Men In Black
By Berthold E. Schwarz, M.D. (Psychiatry)

PUBLISHER'S NOTE:

He was one of the field's most astute researchers, applying his profession in psychiatry to validate the subject of UFOs, but most importantly of those involved in the phenomena itself, as a witness or participant. He counted Howard Menger and Stella Lansing and Betty Hill among those he studied on a professional level. We worked together and shared and number of cases, including this particular MIB episode.

Dr. Berthold Schwarz (Psychiatry), formally of Vero Beach, Florida, was a Diplomat of the American Board of Psychiatry and Neurology and a Fellow of the American Psychiatric Association, among many others. He has contributed over 100 articles to professional journals and has published over a dozen books, including, along with <u>UFO DYNAMICS</u>, <u>Parent-Child Telepathy</u>, <u>The Jacques Romano Story</u>, <u>Psychic-Nexus</u>, <u>You CAN Raise Decent Children</u>, and others.

* * * * *

"Flying Saucer Review" recently published the account of a spectacular possible teleportation, involving two young men in the state of Maine. David Stephens, one of the protagonists, has been involved in some bizarre follow-up experiences which, hopefully, will be fully reported later. This account will be confined to an unusual Man-in-Black (MIB) experience that involved Dr. Herbert Hopkins, the skilled physician who conducted the hypnotic sessions with David Stephens. Dr.

Hopkins is a 58-year-old family physician who lives in a beautiful coastal resort town of Maine.

For the purpose of this report I will try to present the happenings that involved him and other members of his family, using a narrative style based not only on quotations obtained from Mrs. Shirley Fickett's original letters and tapes sent to me shortly after the MIB visitation, but also telephone calls and direct interview with Mrs. Betty Hill who was also involved in the case, numerous telephone and written communications between Dr. Hopkins and me, and taped interviews with Dr. and Mrs. Hopkins, plus a brief meeting with his two sons and daughter-in-law, at his home in Maine, from 1:00 p.m. to 7:30 p.m. on December 1, 1976. . Relevant aspects were also confirmed on interview of Mrs. Hill in Portsmouth, New Hampshire, on November 30, 1976, and an interview of Mrs. Fickeft in Portland, Maine, on the morning of December 1, 1976.

I. Dr. Herbert Hopkin's Experience with a Man in Black

September 11, 1976. Time: 8:00 p.m. Saturday. This was the first time I had been alone in the house for an extended period of time. My wife and children had gone to an outdoor movie, which I dislike.

'The telephone rang and I answered it. A man's voice identified himself as the vice president of the New Jersey UFO Research Organization, and he told me he would like to talk to me about the David Stephens case. He asked if I was entirely alone and if it would be convenient for me to see him. I told him to come right up and I would talk to him. I did not even ask his name, which is very uncharacteristic of me, and also I never see anyone alone since my home and office have been broken into twice and since there is a great deal of illicit drug activity in this town at the present time--even the murder of a pharmacist.

'Immediately I went to the back door to turn on the light so that he could see his way in from my parking lot. Just as I turned on the light, I saw this man dressed in black coming up the porch stairs. I saw no car, and even if he did have a car, he could not have possibly gotten to my house that quickly from *any* phone. Strangely, at the time I did not think of this but opened the door for him without even asking who he was. I do not do things this way ordinarily. He did not introduce himself, but simply came in. He was about 5 feet 8 inches tall and weighed perhaps about 140 pounds. He wore a black derby, a black jacket, black tie, white shirt, black trousers and shoes. I thought, "He looks like an undertaker." I was struck immediately by his immaculate attire. His suit had not a wrinkle and fitted him like a clothing store dummy. It didn't fill out his legs and arms. The crease in his pants was perfect and razor sharp. The suit looked as if he had just put it on. Everything about him seemed to be super-perfect. He asked if he might sit down and I said "Yes." As he sat down, the crease in his trousers even at the knees did not flatten but stood out.

'He removed his hat and I saw that he was completely hairless and had no eyebrows or eyelashes. He had a smooth face with no hair follicles. He had a small nose, set low, and small ears, set low. His head and face were of a dead-white color and his lips were a vivid red in stark contrast to his white face. His eyes were not remarkable – couldn't tell the color, I must have been 12 feet away from him. I remained calm and unafraid as I appraised him. I wonder why? As he asked me about the Stephens case, I noted that he spoke in an expressionless, monotone, scanning speech. His voice--he spoke English, flawless, with no accent, but no sentences, no phrases, just a series of words. His voice was completely neutral and passive.

Men In Black photographed at a New Orleans train station in 2014. Photo courtesy of "outtherewithted.com.

'After I told him about the Stephens case, he said, "That's just what I thought." As I was telling him about the case, he idly put the backs of the fingers of one hand against his lips (he wore gray suede gloves), I noticed that the bright red of his lips had become smeared and the backs of his gloved fingers were stained red! This character was wearing lipstick!

'I thought, "This is some kind of a queer." His mouth was a perfectly straight slit, which he hardly opened. I didn't see any teeth. His head seemed to blend into his collar. He had a receding chin, and he did not move his head at any time; he didn't turn his head, nod, or anything. His head was perfectly stationary with the upper part of his body. As a matter of fact, I'd say with his entire body, except his legs.

'He then told me that I had two coins in my left pocket, which was true, a dime and a penny. He told me to take one of the coins and hold it out in the palm of my open hand. I took the penny because it was the larger of the two coins. Perhaps a 25-cent piece would have been better. I placed the shiny new penny on the palm of my extended hand and looked towards the strange man. He said, "Don't look at me, look at the coin." I did, and the shiny new penny was now a bright silver color. He told me to keep looking at the coin; as I did so the coin slowly became light blue in color, and then it began to become blurred to my vision. My hand was in sharp focus, but try as I might I could not seem to focus on the silver-blue penny. It became more blurred, became round like a little blue fuzzy ball, and then became vaporous and gradually faded away. All the time this was going on I felt and heard nothing. I looked at him and said, "That was a neat trick." I felt eerie at this and asked him to make the coin return. He said, "Neither you nor anyone else on this *plane* (not planet) will ever see that coin again."

'He then asked me if I knew why Barney Hill died, and I told him that I assumed it was the result of a long illness. He told me that this was not the case, that Barney Hill died because he knew too much. He then asked me if I knew how Barney Hill had died, and I told him I understood that he died of a heart attack (wrong information, I was to find out later). He then told me that this was not correct, that he had died because he had no heart, just as I no longer have a coin. This frightened me. He then told me that I had tape recordings of the Stephens case and also correspondence relating to this case. I said that this was true. He then ordered me to destroy the tapes and any other correspondence and literature I might have pertaining to UFOs in any way, or I would suffer the same fate as Barney Hill. He said he would know when I had done this, but did not say that he would come back.

'As he spoke his last words, I noticed that his speech was slowing down. Slowly, and a bit unsteadily, he got to his feet and said, very slowly, "My energy is running low—must go now - goodbye." He walked in four steps to the door and I opened it for him. He clung tightly to the railing as he went down the steps, one foot at a time—one foot down, then the other next to it, before taking the next step—not one foot after another. I watched him as he very unsteadily and slowly walked to the corner of the building and the driveway. He was so unsteady I thought he might fall. I saw a very bright light shining up the driveway and thought that it must be coming from his car--but there was no light there when he arrived. The light was definitely brighter than automobile headlights and was bluish-white in color. I immediately rushed to the nearby kitchen window and looked out to watch him, but I didn't see or hear anything and the light was gone. I rushed out to the front porch but saw no car leaving.

'He walked in a different direction from the driveway—80 degrees opposed to the direction that he came in. I can't remember seeing his shadow. And walking out that way there is no way we could get out because the house is on one side of the driveway and the hedge on the other. The hedge is dense and he'd have a hard time getting through it, especially in his weakened condition. When he didn't appear there, I went out the front door on to the front porch and stood there looking for some time, watching the driveway, waiting for him to come out, but he didn't appear, and no car left the driveway. Two or three cars passed by on the street in the meantime, and I didn't think to look up.

I was much shaken and left all the lights on. The interview took only a matter of minutes. Oh, I don't know—twenty minutes. At no time was there any odor. When the man came to my house, the dog (half shepherd and half collie) barked, then put his tail between his legs, and hid in the closet (unusual behavior). A mother cat and four newborn kittens and a Persian cat were apparently not affected.

'When my two sons and wife returned from the drive-in movie, about one and one-half hours later, I told them of this experience. My oldest boy suggested we examine the driveway for marks and he got a flashlight. We went out and found in the very middle of the driveway a series of marks that looked like a small caterpillar tractor tread. The marks were about four inches wide and continued for only about a foot and a half. There was nothing except this single set of marks. No automobile could have possibly made them because the driveway is too narrow for a car to get over far enough so that its wheels would be in the middle of the driveway. Also, they were too deep and distinct to have been made by a motorcycle, and, also, they did not continue for any length greater than that mentioned above. The marks were gone the next day (no one had used the driveway in the meantime).

'We went back inside and my family urged me to do as the man said. I erased the four tapes and then physically destroyed them in the fireplace. I burned some articles on UFOs and believe I had cleaned out everything. I called Shirley Fickett and asked her to contact the "*National Enquirer*" and tell them not to publish anything (on the Stephens case). Oh, how I hated to destroy those tapes. They weren't hurting anyone, but I wanted to be safe and I was really terrified at this point. I slept well that night, but a week later I had recurring nightmares in which I would see this creature's face getting bigger and closer. The nightmares stopped after a week and have not returned. We have had a lot of trouble since with the telephone being cut off, clicks followed by background sounds indicating that there was an open line to another telephone somewhere, but never any voices. Also, people kept breaking in on phone calls. At the present time, however, the phone has not been disturbed any more. I hope this is the end!'

Mrs. Madeline Hopkins, R.N, the physician's wife, and their two sons and daughter-in-law, verified the account. Mrs. Hopkins recalled how surprised her two sons and she were when they returned home: "All the lights were on—on the porch, the front room, everywhere. I said that something was going on, so John (son) came in to find out. We saw my husband at the table which had a gun on it. I asked what went on? He started telling us the story. I said, "Well, what good was the gun if he made a penny disappear?" I wish I had been there. But then, if I had been there, I don't think he (MIB) would have come.'

II. Strange man and woman visit Dr. Hopkins son and daughter-in-law

Dr. Hopkins continued: 'Here is a transcript of the strange case of John and Maureen Hopkins, my eldest son and his wife.

'Friday, September 24, 1976. Time of phone call 7:30 p.m. (dark). Weather: clear, dry and cool. Air quiet. Phone answered by Maureen.

Conversation: name given as Bill Post. Party calling knew her name, and called her by her name, said he was the friend of a friend who knew John, but did not state who that person was. He stated that they were from Conway, New

Hampshire, and were at King's department store in Biddeford. He asked if they were busy and if they were alone, and he wanted to know if he and his companion could come to visit. There was a pronounced buzzing on the phone and the man's voice sounded distorted. He wanted to know where they could meet and asked, "Isn't there a McDonald's (fast food restaurant) close by you?" He said he was at King's shopping center and that he could get there in five minutes. This would be impossible even under ideal conditions; also, this was a Friday evening and the traffic on U.S. Route 1 was very slow and congested in this area. It would take at least 25 to 30 minutes at this time and under these conditions to get from King's to McDonald's. He said he would recognize John's white van. (John's white van was disabled, in the garage, and he was using his mother's green Chevy, which the man did not know about.)

'It took John three minutes to get to McDonald's as it is quite close. When John drove into McDonald's a young man walked over to him and said, "Hi, John." The window was down and he extended his hand into the car to shake John's hand. He had previously described his car to Maureen over the phone and said it had temporary New Jersey plates on it. John recognized the car as described and noticed that it did have temporary New Jersey plates, but the plates were devoid of any letters or numbers, merely saying: "Temporary, N.J., 1975." The man asked John where could they talk, and John suggested their mobile home. John asked the man to follow him, but they got separated due to a traffic light changing. John slowed down and saw the man's car cutting across the parking lot, going in back of the building, and coming out the driveway and stopping right in back of him. Evidently this person was very familiar with the territory and knew how to take a shortcut and to circumvent the red light. The car followed John to his mobile home.

'The man had a female companion. They were both Caucasian and appeared to be in their mid-thirties. He was about 5 feet 8 inches tall, medium build, about 160 pounds. He had dark hair, but short and smoothly slicked down, a style not seen for many years. He wore a tan, short-sleeved shirt with matching buttons, open at the collar, no tie. His trousers were dark brown, neatly pressed, and had wide cuffs. Style of shoes was not noticed. He wore dark-rimmed glasses. His nose was small with two nostrils, brown normal-appearing eyes, medium-size ears set far back. His voice was high-pitched and had a nasal quality. His complexion was light. He was very talkative without really saying much of anything, and he was quite fidgety.

A pair of Men-In-Black were spotted on security cameras entering the lobby of the Sheraton Hotel at Niagara Falls, New York in 2009.

'His woman companion was about 5 feet 8 inches tall, 150 to 160 pounds, with a pronounced potbelly. She had small, firm breasts, set very low, below the costal margin, and wore no bra. She wore a plain white blouse, black and white checked skirt of an unknown material (seemed it may have been plastic), nylon stockings, black shoes, the slip-on type with small heels which we do not see now. She talked very little, with a whiting voice. She had excessive makeup by today's standards, including very red lips. When she stood up, she seemed quite off-center in relation to the way her legs seemed to join her hips. She walked with very short steps as did her male companion, and leaned forward as though she might fall. She wore no glasses, and her blue eyes appeared to be normal: her nose had a sharp pointed ridge. She had small ears set well back, and very light blonde hair pulled back in a bun. Both presented a rather old-fashioned appearance, perhaps of 20 or more years ago.

"When John and the strangers arrived, Maureen was looking at a Jacques Cousteau underwater TV show which was still on. The man commented that the type of submarine being used was elementary. He downgraded it and indicated that the underwater work being shown was child's play.

'Then while Maureen was in the kitchen, and he was alone with them, John asked them to sit down. The man turned to the girl and said, "Yes, Jane, I guess we can sit down for a little while, can't we?" John asked them if they would like something to drink (non-alcoholic), and the man answered, "We don't drink, take drugs, or anything." John then said that he meant soft drinks like Coca Cola. Both accepted Cokes but did not even taste them.

The man asked John if he watched TV much and what he watched. The man and his companion seemed startled when John told them that both he and his wife watched TV frequently. It was difficult for John to explain to them that he and his wife did most things together. The man said that he knew where John's father lived and asked him if he talked to his father very much and what they talked about. He kept at this point, asking: "Well, did you talk about anything else?" He never got to the point of the three-letter-word I choose not to mention.

'He then said, "The sky is very clear tonight," and said, "You are going to be in amateur radio [no equipment visible, but John, like his father, was involved]. What are you going to use your transmitter for?" When John told him, he asked, "Is that all?" He asked what kind of literature John and Maureen read. John told him that they read many different things but did not elaborate, and the visitor answered, "Yes, I know."

'John went into the kitchen where Maureen was preparing something to eat and asked her to come back with him because he did not want to be alone. Reluctantly she joined them. The man asked John what he did and John told him he was a musician, and the visitor seemed puzzled. While questioning John, he kept pawing and fondling his female companion while repeatedly asking John if it was all right to do this and if he was doing it right.

'John left the room to answer the phone, and the man asked Maureen to sit beside him on the couch, but she refused. While John was on the phone, the man also asked Maureen how she was made. She said, "Oh, what do you mean?" He said, "I mean, how are you built?" She answered: "Well, I guess I'm built just like any other girl." Then he asked her if she had any nude pictures of herself so he could see how she was built and to study the pictures. She was upset and refused, saying, "Certainly not," that she had none. John returned to the room and that was the end of that part of the conversation.

'The man said to John: "You are going to New Jersey." John did have plans to go to New Jersey, but he had not said so to this couple. The man told him to forget the route that the Automobile Club had given to him and that he would tell him how to get there. He then told of a detailed and complicated way to get to New Jersey, which avoided turnpikes and other well-traveled ways and, instead, used all out-of-the way back roads and numerous detours. Later, out of curiosity, John tried to check out some of these roads and found some of them discontinued, some of them rerouted, and some of them no longer considered back roads but now improved main roads.

'That was the end of the visit. The female stood up and said she wanted to leave. Her male companion also stood up but did not start to leave. She repeated to him several times that she wanted to leave, but he did not move. Finally, she said to John, in apparent desperation: "Please move him; I can't move him myself." He was standing closer to the door than she was, but not blocking her exit.

'John finally said, "Well, I think you'd better go now," and tried to calm her down. There were no obstacles--he, she, and the door were in direct line, and apparently the only way she could go to the door was to go directly to it through him: he had to move. The man seemed to want to sit down again, but suddenly left, followed by the female, walking a perfectly straight line, exactly over the spot where he had been standing. They didn't even say goodbye.

'My oldest son had not been able to sleep for a week prior to this visit and for a week after that. I prescribed some Dalmane for him. He said it didn't do much good. However, there was no apparent effect on my other son, wife, or daughter-in-law. Approximately a few weeks after the visit, the man telephoned and spoke to Maureen. He apologized for anything he might have done that seemed inappropriate or out of place, or if they didn't like the way he acted. He was sorry for that and said it wouldn't happen again. He asked if they could please talk some more. However, Maureen just cut him off by saying she didn't want anything to do with people like them.'

From *UFO DYNAMICS: Psychiatric and Psychic Dimensions of the UFO Syndrome* - by Berthold Schwarz, M.D. (Psychiatry)

Reprinted with the permission of Rainbow Books, *Copyright 1983, 1989 by Berthold Eric Schwarz*

FOOTNOTE:

BERTHOLD E. SCHWARZ Berthold E. Schwarz, MD, 85, of Vero Beach, Florida and Green Pond, New Jersey, died Thursday, September 16, 2010 at VNA Hospice House. Born in Jersey City, NJ on October 20, 1924, Dr Schwarz was a proud veteran of the United States Navy. Dr Schwarz received his A.B. from Dartmouth College in 1945 and graduated from Dartmouth Medical School and the N.Y. University College of Medicine in 1950. He interned at Mary Hitchcock Memorial Hospital, Hanover, NH and then completed a Fellowship in Psychiatry at the Mayo Graduate School of Medicine 1951-1955. He also received a M.S. in Psychiatry at the University of Minnesota. Certified in Psychiatry by the American Board of Psychiatry and Neurology, he was a Fellow of the American Psychiatric Association and a member of various other medical and scientific organizations.

After spending nearly 25 years in private practice in Montclair, NJ he moved to Vero Beach in 1982 and continued in private practice for over 20 years. In addition to being a long- time member of the Academy of Spirituality and Paranormal Studies, he was also a Fellow of the American Society for Psychical Research, a Fellow of the American Association for The Advancement of Science, and a Distinguished Life Fellow of the American Psychiatric Association. Dr. Schwarz was also a Diplomate of the American Board of Psychiatry and Neurology and a Fellow of the American Psychiatric Association, among many others. He has authored over 185 scholarly or scientific articles, including many in the Journal of Spirituality and Paranormal Studies. Dr Schwarz also published a number of articles on psychiatric, psychoanalytic and electrophysiological subjects. He contributed to professional journals and published over a dozen books including *"A Psychiatrist Looks at ESP"*. Among his books are *"The Jacques Romano Story"*; *"Psychic Nexus: Psychic Phenomena in Psychiatry"* and *"Everyday Life; Parent-Child Telepathy"*; *"Miracles of Peter Sugleris"*; *"Psychiatric and Paranormal Aspects of Ufology"*; and *"UFO- Dynamics"*.

Has the military signed a secret treaty with the Ultra-Terrestrials that gives us alien technology in exchange for the abduction of humans?

CHAPTER 2

Exposing the Top Secret Treaty Between the U.S. and Aliens

By Sean Casteel

Global Communications/Inner Light Publications, the ever-prolific publishing house helmed by CEO Timothy Green Beckley, has recently published a new book that delves into UFOs, conspiracy theory and governmental gamesmanship called *"America's Top Secret Treaty With Alien Life Forms: Plus The Hidden History of Our Time."* The primary text of the book is by "Commander X," the pseudonym of a former military intelligence operative who has long been dedicated to exposing the government/ET cover-up, but what follows are excerpts and quotations from the book that borrow from the introductory chapters authored by Beckley and, in the interest of full disclosure, myself.

THE NECESSARY LEAPS OF FAITH

To better appreciate the material presented here, one should perhaps make the following leaps of faith:

First, you have to accept the premise that we are not alone in the universe.

Then you have to agree intelligent life has arrived here and that it consists of a group or groups of ETs who are more advanced than we are and who can travel freely through time and space.

Then we must ask ourselves if we are important enough that they would endeavor to set up some sort of ongoing "relationship" with us...and why, indeed, the United States? Could it be because we are thought of as the most powerful nation on the planet?

UFO SPIN DOCTORS

There is a growing conviction among a certain "fringe" group of Ufologists that we have gone so far as to negotiate a treaty with at least one group of aliens, possibly several.

So who signed this treaty? And what exactly does it consist of?

And – perhaps most important of all – has the treaty been broken because one or both sides did not keep to this agreement?

"America's Top Secret Treaty With Alien Life Forms"

EISENHOWER ESTABLISHES FIRST CONTACT

Most stories about the alleged treaty between the U.S. government and a race of UFO occupants start with then President Dwight D. Eisenhower and his rendezvous with the alien interlopers circa 1954.

The story is told in varying versions and may already be familiar in one form or another to the seasoned UFO reader, but it is told again here to lay the foundation for the basic concept of this book. One of the most thorough treatments of the Eisenhower encounter is told by Michael E. Salla, Ph.D., in an online posting called, aptly enough, "Eisenhower's 1954 Meeting With Extraterrestrials."

The chronology begins on the night of, and the early morning hours of February 20-12, 1954, when Eisenhower was purportedly on vacation in Palm Springs and "went missing." The next morning, at a church service in Los Angeles, reporters were told that the president had required emergency dental treatment from a local dentist after losing a tooth cap while eating fried chicken. The dentist himself was presented at an official function that evening, seemingly to solidify an apparent cover-up and keep the press in the dark.

"That missing night and morning," Salla writes, "has subsequently fueled rumors that Eisenhower was using the alleged dentist visit as a cover story for an extraordinary event."

The event is possibly "the most significant that any American president could have conducted," Salla's paper continues. "An alleged 'first contact' meeting with extraterrestrials at Edwards Air Force Base (previously Muroc Airfield) and the beginning of a series of meetings with different extraterrestrial races that led to a 'treaty' that was eventually signed."

Salla then points to circumstantial evidence that the meeting truly occurred. One of the most questionable aspects of situation has to do with Eisenhower's Palm Springs winter vacation itself, slated to run from February 17-24. The vacation was announced rather suddenly and came less than a week after Eisenhower's "quail shooting" vacation in Georgia. This was most unusual.

On the night of February 20, when Eisenhower's presence could not be accounted for, the media began to wonder if he had taken ill or even died. Eisenhower's press secretary quickly convened a news conference and put out the dentist story. During those hours, Eisenhower could easily have traveled from Palm Springs to the nearby Muroc Airfield.

Did Eisenhower meet with aliens at Muroc AFB in the California desert?

When one looks at the unscheduled nature of the president's vacation, the hours he was missing and the dentist cover story, a definite pattern emerges. Whatever was really happening behind the scenes was not something that could be shared with the public.

GERALD LIGHT PROVIDES AN EARLY PUBLIC SOURCE

Gerald Light, who was called a "gifted and highly educated writer and lecturer, skilled in both clairvoyance and the occult," sent a letter dated April 16, 1954, to Meade Layne, who at the time was the director of Borderland Sciences Research Associates.

Light says he witnessed five separate and distinct types of alien aircraft provided by ET's Light called the "Etherians."

In the letter, Light claimed that he was part of a delegation of community leaders invited to the meeting with extraterrestrials at Muroc in order to test public reaction to the alien presence. Also asked to attend were Hearst papers reporter Franklin Allen, Edwin Nourse of the Brookings Institute (who had been Harry Truman's financial adviser), and Bishop MacIntyre of Los Angeles.

After undergoing six hours of "vetting," or extremely detailed background checks, the group was permitted to enter the "restricted section."

"I had the distinct feeling," Light writes, "that the world had come to an end with fantastic realism. For I have never seen so many human beings in a state of complete collapse and confusion, as they realized that their own world had indeed ended with such finality as to beggar description."

This is what the late Harvard psychiatrist Dr. John Mack called "ontological shock." Mack coined the phrase to describe the feeling one gets when first coming to realize the alien presence is undeniably real and that a total restructuring of one's former sense of reality is demanded. Light seems to be describing that shaken state of mind in his letter, which points to a consistency with what the UFO research of the ensuing decades would uncover.

"The reality of the 'other plane' aero-forms is now and forever removed from the realms of speculation," Light continued, "and made a rather painful part of the consciousness of every responsible scientific and political group."

Light says he was on the scene at Muroc for two days and witnessed five separate and distinct types of alien aircraft being studied and handled by Air Force officials with the permission and assistance of a group Light calls the "Etherians."

"I have no words to express my reactions," he writes. "It has finally happened. It is now a matter of history."

Light mistakenly felt that Eisenhower would ignore the conflicts going on between various officials behind the scenes and present the situation to the public if the impasse continued much longer. Salla notes that no such formal announcement was made and Light's meeting was either the best-kept secret of the 20th century or the fabrication of an elderly mystic known for out-of-body experiences.

Meanwhile, Salla says there is plausibility to the list of those Light claimed had joined him at the meeting in that they represented senior leaders of the religious, spiritual, economic and newspaper communities. All of the invitees were of advanced age and constituted a "wise man" group that would have reflected the conservative nature of American society at the time.

WILLIAM COOPER ADDS ANOTHER LAYER OF CREDENCE

The late William Cooper was a highly controversial whistleblower of great fame, though his statements would often be critically scrutinized and attacked. As for his personal background, he said he served on the Naval Intelligence briefing team for the Commander of the Pacific Fleet from 1970 to 1973 and therefore had access to classified documents that he had to review in order to fulfill his briefing duties.

According to Salas, Cooper describes the background and nature of the "First Contact" thusly:

"In 1953, astronomers discovered large objects in space which were moving toward the Earth. It was first believed that they were asteroids. Later evidence proved that the objects could only be spaceships. When the objects reached the Earth, they took up a very high orbit around the Equator. There were several huge ships, and their actual intent was unknown."

Operatives of Project Sigma, which worked to intercept radio signals, and a new project, Plato, tasked with establishing diplomatic relations with this race of space aliens, worked together to transmit radio communications to the ships using the binary computer language. The U.S. was thus able to arrange a landing that resulted in face-to-face contact with alien beings from another planet. In the meantime, a race of human-looking aliens also contacted the U.S. government.

"This alien group warned us against the aliens that were orbiting the Equator and offered to help us with our spiritual development. They demanded that we dismantle our nuclear weapons as the major condition. They refused to exchange technology citing that we were spiritually unable to handle the technology which we then possessed. They believed that we would use any new technology to destroy each other."

This race stated that:

*** We were on a path of self-destruction and we must stop killing each other.

*** We must stop polluting the Earth.

*** We must stop raping the Earth's natural resources.

*** We must learn to live in harmony.

Cooper writes that these terms were met with extreme suspicion, especially the major condition of nuclear disarmament. It was believed that meeting that condition would leave us helpless in the face of an obvious alien threat. We also

William Cooper would broadcast to the world every day via shortwave radio.

had no precedent in history to help in making the decision. In any case, it was decided that nuclear disarmament was not in the best interest of the United States. The aliens' overtures were rejected.

"The significant point about Cooper's version," Salla writes, "is that the humanoid extraterrestrial race was not willing to enter into technology exchanges that might help weapons development and was instead focused on spiritual development. Significantly, the overtures of these extraterrestrials were turned down."

In retrospect, it seems we said "no" to the good guys, doesn't it?

THE 1954 AGREEMENT WITH THE ALIENS

Did the aliens engage us early on, insisting we sign a Treaty with them? If so, have they led us down the garden path?

A host of other whistleblowers, to include former CIA pilot John Lear and former Master Sergeant Robert Dean (who, like Cooper, had access to top secret documents) offer accounts of the Muroc meeting that agree on some points and disagree on others,

In any case, Eisenhower's February 1954 meeting was not successful. After the failure of that first meeting, the president subsequently met later that year with a race of large-nosed gray aliens who had been orbiting the Earth before landing at Holloman Air Force Base in New Mexico.

Eisenhower and/or members of his administration reached a basic agreement with this second alien race. The ETs identified themselves as originating from a planet in orbit around a red star in the Constellation of Orion that we call Betelgeuse. They stated that their planet was dying and that at some unknown future time they would no longer be able to survive there.

The treaty reached with this gray race stated that the aliens would not interfere in our affairs and we would not interfere in theirs. We would keep their presence on Earth a secret. They would furnish us with advanced technology and would help us in our technological development.

They would not make a treaty with any other Earth nation.

They could abduct humans on a limited and periodic basis for the purposes of medical examination and the monitoring of our development, with the stipulation that the humans would not be harmed, would be returned to their point of abduction, and would have no memory of the event. The alien nation agreed to furnish a list of all human contacts and abductees on a regularly scheduled basis.

Further testimony comes from yet another whistleblower, Phil Schneider, a former geological engineer who was employed by corporations contracted to build underground bases. Schneider worked extensively on black projects involving extraterrestrials. He summarized what he knew about the earthling/alien compact:

"Back in 1954, under the Eisenhower administration, the federal government decided to circumvent the Constitution of the United States and form a treaty with alien entities. It was called the 1954 Greada Treaty, which basically made the agreement that the aliens involved could take a few cows and test their implanting techniques on a few human beings but that they had to give details about the people involved."

This same pattern of testimony is also repeated by Don Phillips, who served in the Air Force on various clandestine aviation projects. He claims to have seen documents detailing the facts of Eisenhower's meeting with the aliens and the fact that some kind of treaty was later signed.

Meanwhile, the late Colonel Philip Corso, a highly decorated officer who had served on Eisenhower's National Security Council and decades later authored the highly controversial book, "The Day After Roswell," characterized what had happened as a kind of "negotiated surrender" to the aliens. Corso wrote in his memoirs that "They dictated the terms because they knew what we most feared was disclosure."

THE ALIENS PROVE UNTRUSTWORTHY

The whistleblowers also talked about the immediate aftermath of the treaty.

"By 1955," Cooper writes, "it became obvious that the aliens had deceived Eisenhower and had broken the treaty. It was suspected that the aliens were not submitting a complete list of human contacts and abductees and it was further suspected that not all abductees had been returned."

Lear says similarly, "We got something less than the technology we bargained for and found the abductions exceeded by a million-fold what we had naively agreed to."

In October 1955, General Douglas MacArthur delivered a famous warning that suggested some extraterrestrial presence existed that threatened human sovereignty.

"You now face a new world," MacArthur said, "a world of change. We speak in strange terms, of harnessing the cosmic energy, of ultimate conflict between a united human race and the sinister forces of some other planetary galaxy. The nations of the world will have to unite, for the next war will be an interplanetary war. The nations of the Earth must someday make a common front against attack by people from other planets."

MacArthur may well have been alluding to the same extraterrestrials who allegedly made an agreement with Eisenhower. It is a public acknowledgment, similar to Ronald Reagan's "little green man" speech before the United Nations in 1983, of an alien presence against whom the entire planet must one day do battle. If the aliens did in fact renege on major parts of the alleged treaty, MacArthur was perhaps acknowledging that we would eventually be in a state of all-out war with them as a consequence.

"The uncertainty over the motivations and behavior of the gray extraterrestrials," Salla writes, "appears to have played a large role in the government decision not to disclose the extraterrestrial presence and the treaty Eisenhower had signed with them."

Salla quotes from an "alleged official document" leaked to UFO researchers that makes it a crime under the Espionage Act to disclose classified information concerning extraterrestrials, punishable by up to ten years in prison and a $10,000 fine. Which is sufficient to keep most former servicemen from coming forward with what they know. The most common strategies for dealing with former servicemen, corporate employees or witnesses brave or "foolish" enough to reveal classified information is to intimidate, silence, eliminate or discredit these individuals. This is accomplished by removing all public records of the whistleblowers that would establish their identity as credible sources. Such people could also be frightened into simply retracting what they said or having their testimony distorted to the point where it ceases to have the meaning the witness intended.

EISENHOWER AS THE "CONTACTEE" PRESIDENT

Returning to the subject of Eisenhower and the many alien contact stories that are told about him, we next examine the writings of Canadian researcher Grant Cameron. Cameron has specialized in the study of American presidents and their interactions with the extraterrestrial presence for many years and has cultivated a reputation for reliability and trustworthiness that has few equals in the field of Ufology.

According to Cameron, Eisenhower's attaining the rank of five-star General made him accustomed to high-level secrets. This was clearly evident in 1952, when Harry Truman gave the newly elected Eisenhower the "comprehensive National Intelligence Digest prepared by the CIA," which contained "the most important national intelligence on a worldwide basis." Eisenhower would write in his memoirs a decade later that the intelligence digest added little to his knowledge since he had already been privy to most of what it contained.

"What may go down as the most contentious part of the Eisenhower story," Cameron writes, "is that Eisenhower had many rumored encounters with UFOs and aliens. Eisenhower could thus be labeled the 'contactee president.'"

Eisenhower was said to be onboard a nuclear aircraft carrier in 1952 during a NATO exercise in which a large blue/white light appeared right off the starboard bow. It descended to within a hundred feet above the water and hovered as the ship moved past it before rising straight up into the air and departing. Eisenhower told the crewmen to "forget about it for now."

The ship in question was the U.S.S. Roosevelt. Cameron points out that just as Roswell was the first air force base to handle nuclear weapons, the U.S.S. Roosevelt was the first aircraft carrier to be armed with nuclear weapons. There has been a generally acknowledged alien "interest" in Earth's nukes from the beginning of the modern day UFO phenomenon, and one is reminded that the aliens who initially approached Eisenhower made dismantling our nuclear arsenal a fundamental condition of any agreement that might be reached.

Cameron also comments on the 1954 Muroc story. Ever the careful scholar, Cameron relates how the official records of the President's trip to Palm Springs are held at the Eisenhower library in Abilene, Kansas, and have been reviewed by various researchers. An archivist at the library says they receive so many requests on the subject that they have a person who specializes in dealing with those particular documents.

"All researchers agreed on the basic story," Cameron writes, "that being on the evening of February 20, 1954, during a weeklong trip to Palm Springs, Eisenhower disappeared from where he was staying at the Smoke Tree Ranch compound. The records do not show how this disappearance became apparent to the press corps, but they did figure out the president was gone. In fact, the Associated Press had already gone on the wire with the story that the president had suffered a heart attack and was dead. Minutes later, they withdrew the story."

Press secretary James Haggerty hurried to meet with the press with the aforementioned dentist visit story. The members of the media accepted what they were told when Eisenhower was seen at church the next morning.

WHAT EISENHOWER SAID PUBLICLY

In his introduction to *"America's Top Secret Treaty With Alien Life Forms,"* Beckley grapples with statements Eisenhower made to the American public shortly before turning over the reins of government to John F. Kennedy – the well-known remarks on the military/industrial complex.

"In the councils of government," Eisenhower said, "we must guard against the acquisition of unwarranted influence, whether sought or unsought, by the military/industrial complex. The potential for the disastrous rise of misplaced power exists and will persist. We must never let the weight of this combination endanger our liberties or democratic processes. We should take nothing for granted. Only an alert and knowledgeable citizenry can compel the proper meshing of the huge industrial and military machinery of defense with our peaceful methods and goals, so that security and liberty may prosper together.

If Eisenhower did have a clandestine meeting with aliens, what was the result of their conversation? What were the discussions all about?

"To all the peoples of the world," the president continued, "I once more give expression to America's prayerful and continuing aspiration: We pray that peoples of all faiths, all races, all nations, may have their great human needs satisfied; that those now denied opportunity will come to enjoy it to the full; that all who yearn for freedom may experience its spiritual blessings; that those who have freedom will understand, also, its heavy responsibilities; that all who are insensitive to the needs of others will learn charity; that the scourges of poverty, disease and ignorance will be made to disappear from the Earth, and that, in the goodness of time, all peoples will come to live together in a peace guaranteed by the binding force of mutual respect and love."

Did the aliens insist we sign a treaty with them? If so, have they violated this treaty?

The surprising candor of Eisenhower's exit speech has long placed it among the most important presidential utterances in American history. But what motivated him to speak his dire warnings about governmental machinery he had himself been a leader of for decades?

"Certainly, these remarks serve to indicate," Beckley writes, "that something during his two terms of office had had a tremendous effect upon a president who was a staunch conservative and a former general not known for his sensitivity and enlightenment. What had impacted his conscience so much that he would publicly 'soften' his views on a variety of topics? Could it have been due to his rumored meeting with a group of Ultra-Terrestrials? And the subsequent fact that these assemblages were never spoken about in public?

"Going a step further," Beckley continues, "if Eisenhower did have a prearranged, clandestine meeting with aliens, what was the result of their conversation? What were the discussions all about? What future policies might they have outlined? And, at the end of the meeting(s), did we simply shake hands and say, 'see you,' as we walked away?

"There are some, including Commander X, the retired military intelligence operative, who say that these conferences with Eisenhower led up to an actual agreement – an interplanetary treaty – being 'signed and sealed' by both sides."

On a personal note, the above-mentioned Commander X is a mystery even to me. I have worked for Beckley (who has published numerous books by Commander X) for more than twenty years and even I do not know who the secretive author truly is. I've always conjured an image of an aging, gray-haired, bearded figure bent over a typewriter while hiding in some basement hovel in a major U.S. city and staying one step ahead of his former intelligence community "handlers" as he churns out book after book on the shadowy conspiracy that allegedly threatens us all. In his section of *America's Top Secret Treaty With Alien Life Forms*, Commander X provides an insider's perspective on the nature of official government dealings and agreements with the aliens.

Is Commander X trustworthy? I would have to say he's at least as trustworthy as the next guy in this often confusing swirl of disinformation and genuinely leaked "revelations."

But whatever the details of this insidious treaty between the U.S. and the extraterrestrials, no matter what was agreed to, what egregious concessions were made, no matter who profited or was enriched, it is we who will pay the final price of that ill-conceived diplomatic outreach to a dark alien race from the stars.

**A UFO hovers over David Bowie.
Courtesy of and © by artist Nicholas May.**

CHAPTER 3

David Bowie – "Starman"

By Timothy Green Beckley

I first met David Bowie during his original tour of the United States when he had adopted the stage persona of "Ziggy Stardust," a sort of lost-in-space androgynous alien, complete with cosmic makeup and a painted lightning bolt zigzagging across his face down to his naked chest.

Before venturing across the pond, Bowie had caused quite a sensation in the British press not only because of his outlandish – to some – image of a rock and roller from Mars, but also because of his independent and very liberal sexual lifestyle.

Bowie was introduced to me at the RCA studios in Manhattan by Walli Elmlark, a bedazzling young lady who wrote a regular column for "Circus Magazine." "Circus" was a sort of heavy metal version of "Rolling Stone" that was printed on glossy paper with color photos of pop star favorites who were emerging on the then-burgeoning glam and glitter rock scenes.

As usual, at the time I was wearing several hats. I was promoting a number of local rock bands who never quite "made it," editing the widely distributed "UFO Review" (the world's only official flying saucer newspaper), and running the New York School Of Occult Arts and Sciences, among the first metaphysical centers in the country where you could take classes in anything from astral projection to hypnosis to witchcraft. Which is how I came to be acquainted with Walli Elmlark. As I originally wrote in *UFOs Among The Stars – Close Encounters of The Famous* (Global Communications), Walli was known widely as the White Witch Of New York. Because of her contacts in the music industry, she had established quite an eclectic clientele for whom she would offer spiritual guidance and occasional good luck or love spells, but always of a positive nature. She didn't dabble in black magick or even gris gris (a New Orleans form of "gray magick" that incorporates poppets and the use of talismans kept in a personal mojo bag). Walli was lively, imaginative, energetic, well spoken, and quite attractive in her flowing white garments complete with fashionable silver moon adornments. Oh did I forget to mention long black hair, complete with dyed green streak highlights? Indeed, Wallie made a very bold fashion and occult statement wherever she went.

BOWIE – THE MAN WHO FELL TO EARTH

Early in life, Bowie had established his interest in all matters extraterrestrial. As a Brit teenager, David had helped edit a flying saucer newsletter. He admitted to me that he loved science fiction and was fascinated with life in space and the possibility that quite a few cosmic visitors had ended up on our earthly shores.

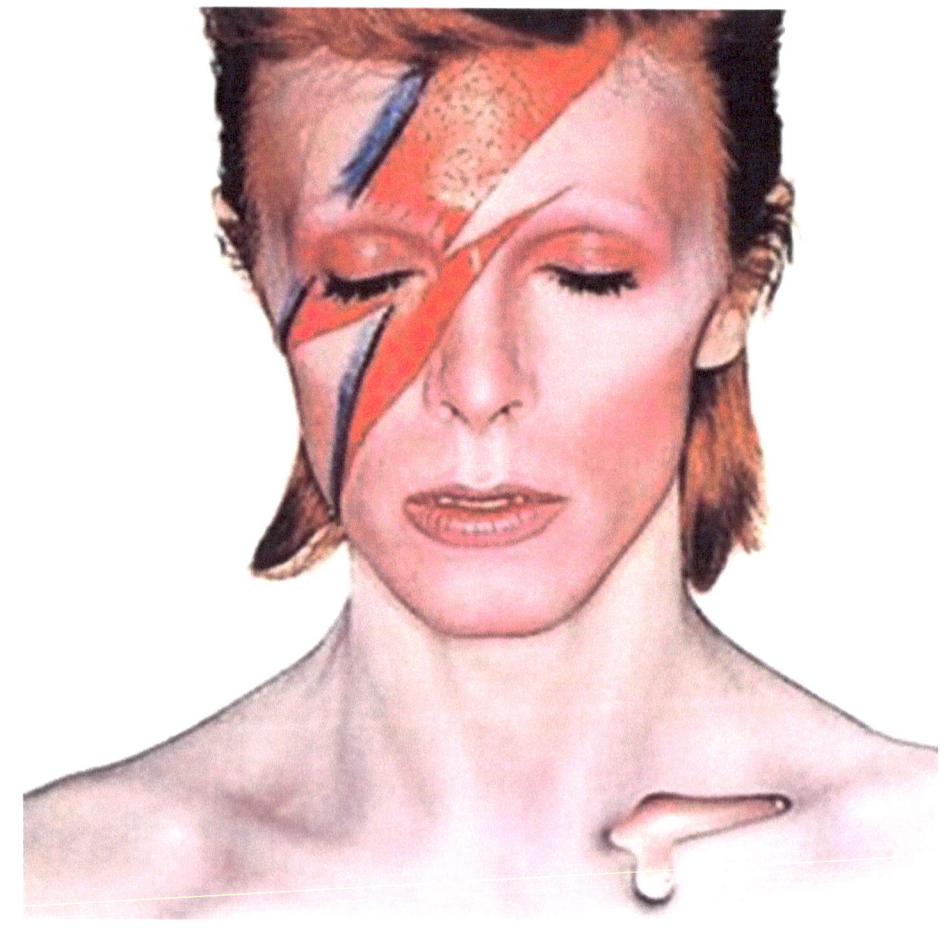

Bowie as Ziggy Stardust.

During a conversation, Bowie had gone out on a limb revealing that he had once had a close encounter. In the book "*Laugh Gnostic,*" author Peter Koening paraphrases what Bowie said: "A friend and I were traveling in the English countryside when we both noticed a strange object hovering above a field. From then on, I have come to take this phenomenon seriously. I believe that what I saw was not the actual object but a projection of my own mind trying to make sense of this quantum topological doorway into dimensions beyond our own. It's as if our dimension is but one among an infinite number of others."

In the February 1975 issue of the long defunct "CREEM Magazine," Bowie seems to admit to a reporter that he might have an implant or metal inside his body. It's hard to define his exact feeling on this, but this is the quote attributed to him by Bruno Stein, the writer who conducted the interview:

"Well, it turned out David was in luck. If he went to a little town in Missouri at a certain time, he would be able to see in a seemingly empty field a fully equipped flying saucer repair shop at work.

"It was one of those fascinating things you learn at a Bowie soiree. This evening the gathering was rather intimate. There was Corinne, David's charming personal secretary, who ducked out early due to exhaustion (although another participant gossiped that she had someone interesting waiting for her in her hotel room). "I used to work for two guys who put out a UFO magazine in England," he told the flying saucer man. "About six years ago. And I made sightings six, seven times a night for about a year when I was in the observatory. We had regular cruises that came over. We knew the 6.15 was coming in and would meet up with another one. And they would be stationary for about half an hour, and then after verifying what they'd been doing that day, they'd shoot off.

"But, I mean, it's what you do with the information. We never used to tell anybody. It was beautifully dissipated when it got to the media. Media control is still based in the main on cultural manipulation. It's just so easy to do. When you set up one set of objectives toward the public and you've given them a certain definition for each code word, you hit them with the various code words and they're not going to believe anything if you don't want them to..."

From his performances, you could tell that nothing was too "non-establishment" for David. He incorporated time machines and space capsules into his act and wrote "A Space Oddity" and talked about how a "Starman" would like to come and visit us, "but he thinks he'd blow our minds." His appeared in the motion picture **"The Man Who Fell To Earth**," which has become a classic. In concert, Bowie was radiant and his fans were floating on a cloud, but behind the scenes an ominous specter was forming from which the master of time and space would quickly need some righteous assistance in order to escape a wall of paranoia that was building around him.

AND ALONG COMES MR. SCRATCH

Like many rockers before and after, David had taken a liking to the good life. You know the old adage: sex, drugs and rock and roll. Well, on top of this, add a heap of consciousness expansion and an interest in the occult and you will have the prevalent influences on what might have seemed like Bowie's immortal being.

But paranoia soon struck in the form of the ole nemesis "nose candy," commonly known as cocaine. With the help of Bowie himself and some close associates at the time, Marc Spitz details in *"Bowie: A Biography"* (Crown) how David was living in L.A. just a few houses away from the estate where Charlie Manson's gang had terribly mutilated Sharon Tate and her friends in a ritualistic murder. Bowie had taken to doing blow regularly and was getting more and more desperate and paranoid with each passing day.

In a number of shocking revelations, biographer Marc Spitz explains precisely what was transpiring in the pop singer's troubled life: "While planning the follow-up to 'Young Americans,' Bowie would sit in the house with a pile of high-quality cocaine atop the glass coffee table, a sketch pad and a stack of books. *'Psychic Self Defense'* (Dion Fortune) was his favorite. Its author describes the book as a 'safeguard for protecting yourself against paranormal malevolence.'

"Using this and more arcane books on witchcraft, white magic and its malevolent counterpart, black magic, as rough guides to his own rapidly fragmenting psyche, Bowie began drawing protective pentagrams on every surface."

Bowie told the author, "I'd stay up for weeks. Even people like Keith Richards were floored by it. And there were pieces of me all over the floor. I paid with the worst manic depression of my life. My psyche went through the roof; it just fractured into pieces. I was hallucinating 24 hours a day."

Spitz adds, "Increasingly Bowie was convinced there were witches after his semen. They were intent on using it to make a child to sacrifice to the devil, essentially the plot to Roman Polanski's 1968 supernatural classic '**Rosemary's Baby**.'"

**A blast from the past - "early" Walli Elmlark.
Photo from the Michael Lawrence Collection.**

Seeing that he was in desperate need, poet and songwriter Cherry Vanilla hooked Bowie up with Walli Elmlark, who Spitz describes as a "Manhattan-based intellectual...who taught classes at the New York School of Occult Arts and Sciences, then located on Fourteenth Street, just north of Greenwich Village." (As mentioned previously, I was the director of the school, which began in the mid-1960s and thrived for more than a decade promoting lectures and classes by the who's who of paranormal and UFO experts of that era, including Cleve Backster, Stanley Krippner, Jim Moseley, John Keel – and, of course, Walli Elmlark, the White Witch of New York.)

As added confirmation of the madness David was trying to cope with, ex-wife Angie Bowie reveals even more details of his fascination and dabbling into the occult in her own personal remembrance, "Backstage Passes: Life on the Wild Side With David Bowie."

"There was a beautiful Art Deco house on six acres, an exquisite site property and a terrific value at just $300,000, but he took one look at a detail I hadn't noticed, a hexagram painted on the floor of a circular room by the previous owner, Gypsy Rose Lee.

UFO SPIN DOCTORS

"A great deal of coddling and reassurance got us through that crisis, and I went and found the Doheny Drive house. Built in the late fifties or early sixties, it was a white cube surrounding an indoor swimming pool. David liked the place, but I thought it was too small to meet our needs for very long, and I wasn't crazy about the pool. In my experience, indoor pools are always a problem.

"This one was no exception, albeit not in any of the usual ways. Its drawback was one I hadn't encountered before and haven't seen or heard of since: Satan lived in it. With his own eyes, David said, he'd seen HIM rising up out of the water one night."

Feeling demonic forces moving in, David felt strongly that he needed an exorcism and asked that his newfound friend, white witch Walli Elmlark, be called upon to lend her assistance to remove the evil from his surroundings.

"A Greek Orthodox Church in L.A. would have done it for us (there was a priest available for such a service, the people had told me), but David wouldn't have it. No strangers allowed, he said. So there we stood, with just Walli's instructions and a few hundred dollars' worth of books, talismans, and assorted items from Hollywood's comprehensive selection of fine occult emporia.

Street level view of home whose pool was possibly possessed by a demon.

"There he (David Bowie) was, then, primed and ready. The proper books and doodads were arranged on a big old-fashioned lectern. The incantation began, and although I had no idea what was being said or what language it was being said in, I couldn't stop a weird cold feeling rising up in me as David droned on and on.

"There's no easy or elegant way to say this, so I'll just say it straight. At a certain point in the ritual, the pool began to bubble. It bubbled vigorously (perhaps 'thrashed' is a better term) in a manner inconsistent with any explanation involving air filters or the like."

The rock and roll couple watched in amazement. Angie says she tried to be flippant – "Well, dear, aren't you clever? It seems to be working. Something's making a move, don't you think?' – But I couldn't keep it up. It was very, very strange; even after my recent experiences I was having trouble accepting what my eyes were seeing."

Angie said that she would peek through the glass doors which lead to the pool every so often and was dumbfounded by what she saw.

"On the bottom of the pool was a large shadow, or stain, which had not been there before the ritual began. It was in the shape of a beast of the underworld; it reminded me of those twisted, tormented gargoyles screaming silently from the spires of medieval cathedrals. It was ugly, shocking, malevolent; it frightened me.

"I backed away from it, feeling very strange, went through the doorway, and told David what I'd seen, trying to be nonchalant but not doing very well. He turned white but eventually became revived enough to spend the rest of the night doing coke. He wouldn't go near the pool, though.

"I still don't know what to think about that night. It runs directly counter to my pragmatism and my everyday faith in the integrity of the 'normal' world, and it confuses me greatly. What troubles me the most is that if you were to call that stain the mark of Satan, I don't see how I could argue with you.

"David, of course, insisted that we move from the house as quickly as possible, and we did that, but I've heard from reliable sources (Michael Lipman for one, the property's real estate agent) that subsequent tenants haven't been able to remove the shadow. Even though the pool has been painted over a number of times, the shadow has always come back."

Bowie's Aleister Crowley influences are showing in this comparison pose.

Several years went by and Walli met an untimely passing. She could not remove the demons in her own life, even though she had a dramatic and positive impact on almost everyone she came in contact with. Besides teaching at the School Of Occult Arts And Sciences, Walli teamed up with the likes of T. Rex's Marc Bolan (whom she nicknamed the Wizzard) and King Crimson's guitarist, Robert Fripp. The trio went off to merry old England to record a spoken word album Though "The Cosmic Children" has never been released, the soundtrack was years ahead of its time, centering on those special souls who Walli believed had reincarnated on Earth from "elsewhere" at a very important time in the human evolutionary process to pass on the light to others who were destined to change the world through music, literature and an emerging New Age philosophy. The recording is out there somewhere – perhaps safely in the vault of Robert Fripp – who, hopefully, if he reads this, will contact me and allow us to do a limited pressing for those who would truly find this effort transformational.

Walli and I worked for a number of years on several projects and even co-authored a book together. Out of print for decades, once in a while I still run across a copy of *"Rock Raps of the Seventies"* offered on e-bay or elsewhere at an exorbitant price.

Somehow, I can't deny the possibility that Walli looks down from time to time and perhaps sings along with David Bowie as he performs all over the world in concert. Long recovered from drugs and the dark aspects of occultism, he is now raising a family and going on with his chosen task. And perhaps, before you know it, his "Starman" song may take on a reality all its own if the predicted disclosure about UFOs and extraterrestrials ever comes about in our lifetime.

Over the years we had heard unsubstantiated rumors that Bowie was intrigued by an incident where a UFO was said to have crashed in the desert. We were never able to pin anything down about this incident until we found out that it was actually scribed by Bowie's original publicist and a longtime friend of ours, Cherry Vanilla, who was in his hotel suite when the story came over the TV. Writing under Bowie's name, this is what the fiery redhead is quoting as having been said under Bowie's name in "Mirabelle," a sort of diary published by Bowie's camp.

"I heard the most incredible thing the other day that I must tell you about, and I promise every single word of it is true! I was in Detroit, where I was due to do a concert, and before the show I was sitting in my hotel room listening to the radio.

"Suddenly, the newsman interrupted the regular program with the news that a spaceship had been found in the desert – an alien spaceship about six feet wide and thirty feet long – and inside were three alien beings. The three creatures were killed on impact when the spaceship plummeted to Earth, but they were taken to a hospital to be examined anyway. These people looked like human beings but were much smaller and, when they were examined, it was discovered that their vital organs were like human beings too! The catch is that their brains were found to be much farther advanced! Wow!

"As soon as the newscast was over, I got the band and my back-up singers together and had them ring up radio and TV stations all over the country to see if they had all got the report. About half the stations said they had and half denied it. So, it really is quite a mystery. No one knows what's happened to the spaceship or the spacemen at this point, and it seems that someone is trying to cover up the whole matter completely!"

And so it goes. And while Bowie has given up his Ziggy Stardust roots he does not seem to have abandoned his interest in UFOs and the Star People which have been such an influence on his career.

Signs and Symbols of the Second Coming, by Sean Casteel.

CHAPTER 4

The Mass Landing Myth and The Arrival of the Armies of God

By Sean Casteel

*(The following is an excerpt from the book, "**Signs and Symbols of the Second Coming, Expanded and Revised Edition**," by Sean Casteel, with additional material by Timothy Green Beckley.)*

There exists a prevailing belief among a great many within the UFO community that there will someday come a "mass landing," a revelation to the entire world of the flying saucer reality we have only seen the briefest hints of so far. We somehow believe we are "owed" a climactic revelation as to the true nature of the flying saucer phenomenon, that we will one day have paid our dues and will receive a payoff in the form of some kind of ultimate truth.

One of the most common ways this idea is expressed is with the phrase "a landing on the White House lawn," which presumes the U.S. president would be the first person the alien presence would want to communicate with. This is sort of an extension of the old 1950s cliché in which the aliens land and say, "Take me to your leader." Perhaps the White House landing myth implies that they have eliminated the middleman/informant and gone straight to what Americans in their national pride would like to assume is the leader of the free world.

Another myth this basic concept incorporates is that of a morally indifferent alien force that wants to talk politics at the White House and eventually be interviewed on CNN. Any number of similar scenarios can be imagined while the waiting for some kind of open disclosure of the alien presence by the UFO occupants themselves continues. We wait, without being able to define what we're waiting for.

But what if we're waiting for the wrong kind of mass landing? What if the UFO occupants are not morally indifferent at all? What if the ancient astronaut interpreters of the phenomenon are right and the aliens are the gods that created us and at least tried to teach mankind a set of moral codes, a system of ethics that reflected their own "alien" morals and ethics? Perhaps the Old Testament word would be "righteousness," and the prophets crying out down through the ages for truth and justice were not merely raving in some kind of sacrosanct psychosis but were, as they claimed, pressed into service as a "mouthpiece" or advocate for God?

There has always been a thin line between madness and genuine religious experience. The story of Abraham and his near-sacrifice of his son Isaac is a frequently used example of this problem. Abraham claims to hear a "voice," which he assumes to be God, telling him to "sacrifice" his son. If Abraham were to walk into a courtroom today and tell a judge his "voices" told him to murder his own child, one would hope he would receive immediate hospitalization. It is typical of the schizophrenic to use what psychiatry would call "religious delusions" to justify any number of violent or otherwise antisocial behaviors.

Yet from childhood we are taught that Abraham was not psychotic and was having a genuine conversation with the true God. We are also taught that God chose at the final instant to take mercy on both Abraham and Isaac, providing a sacrificial animal, seemingly out of nowhere, to substitute for a frightened and confused Isaac. God's real point had been to test Abraham's faith, in a manner appropriate to the historical context of the ancient world.

As UFO believers, we too would like some kind of assurance that we are on the right side of that same thin line. While the morals of this country and the world around us may be said to have deteriorated to a depressing, even dangerous degree, there still exists a kind of social contract, law and order, and an agreed upon effort to maintain a level of ethical behavior we can live with comfortably enough to survive.

We think we know what is right and who among us could somehow trust an invading alien army to tell us different? Would these faceless, unknowable flying saucer occupants necessarily have a moral agenda at all? And should they have such an agenda, would they automatically want to impose that on us or even deign to teach it to us?

The Annunciation, with Saint Emidius. Painted in 1486 by Italian artist Carlo Crivelli, it shows the "Holy Spirit" represented as a UFO-type cloud, shooting a beam of light at the Virgin Mary.

What to fear and who to trust about that fear? These kind of unanswerable questions inevitably grow wearisome to even the hardiest of UFO speculators. But this book on UFOs and the Second Coming is an attempt to answer some of those questions by blending the prophecies of the Bible with what little is known of the UFO phenomenon. Admittedly, in the marketplace of truth as it exists today, we already have two strikes against us. We are taking up two sharp sticks of something society has seen numerous examples of in the context of insanity – Biblical prophecy and UFOs – and giving ourselves a painful poke in the eye. Many a maniac with an axe to grind has wrapped himself in one or both of these subjects, usually to nauseating effect.

But nevertheless, we persist in this line of inquiry, of careful painstaking research. I have interviewed a group of experts on the subjects of Biblical prophecy and UFOs. Some have made the leap of faith and believe they are two inseparable parts of an overall whole, while other interviewees quoted here tend to carefully avoid expressing a belief in some future violent apocalypse.

For instance, what does the Second Coming mean to ordained minister Dr. Barry Downing? Downing's impressive academic background in both science and religion, combined with a longtime study of the UFO phenomenon, makes his opinion as "expert" as they come.

Biblical prophecy scholar Gary Stearman discusses how the long awaited Rapture will be timed to events in Israel and explains how UFO waves in that embattled stretch of Earth have always been an expression of God's unfolding plan in the modern world. One must learn to live with the idea that the Day of the Lord will arrive as a "thief in the night," catching the entire world off-guard and entering our reality unannounced.

There are also chapters offering the aforementioned less apocalyptic view of the Second Coming. In interviews with religious and UFO scholar Dr. Brenda Denzler and prophecy researcher G.C. Schellhorn, Christ's return is portrayed as a quieter transformation of humankind's collective consciousness, a kind of moral rebirth taking place on levels too subtle to be readily apparent to the unenlightened observer. What if Christ and the other prophets can achieve their merciful ends without a "blood and guts" confrontation with the wickedness of the world?

The legendary husband and wife team of Brad and Sherry Steiger are interviewed for separate chapters about their beliefs on the Second Coming. Brad recalls his youthful days in Bible class and explains how his views are now less extreme, less black and white, regarding what we mean when we discuss things like the fearful aspects of the Book of Revelation.

Meanwhile, Sherry also feels her childhood religious beliefs and even time spent in a Lutheran seminary as a young woman did not prepare her for the truths she would later discover. What should be emphasized, she believes, is the commonality between all world faiths and the peaceful, good intentions of the prophets who introduced them to us. Yet she concedes she is troubled by portions of Book of Revelation and believes the Mark of the Beast could easily become a reality. Read her chapter in *"Signs and Symbols of the Second Coming"* to find out why.

Did the late Dr. Frank Stranges correctly identify the Antichrist? He is among the many who have tried to "name names" in that regard, but in this exclusive interview he explains his reasoning for doing so in some detail, while at the same time decrying the "fear mongers" who use the Second Coming to terrify rather than to inspire. Will the UFOs eventually spread the wisdom and grace of Christianity to the entire universe after carrying out the Second Coming on Earth?

Finally, I touch on the possible use of holograms to stage a false Second Coming and offer a checklist of signs to watch for in the countdown to the Day of the Lord, as provided by Gray Stearman.

Returning to the subject that began this chapter, it is my belief that we should not be waiting for a morally indifferent landing on the White House lawn. Should the mass landing come, it will more likely be from the skies over Armageddon, when the UFOs arrive en masse to combat the armies gathered by the Antichrist. Jesus Christ is often thought of as the teacher who cautioned us to turn the other cheek but he also said he came not to bring peace but the sword. In Revelation, Chapter 19, he is called the Word of God, he from whose mouth issues a sharp sword with which he smites the nations. He is accompanied by the "armies of heaven" who follow behind him on white horses. Would you not agree that all that stands in marked contrast to "moral indifference"?

In a book published by Tim Beckley's Inner Light Publications, called *"Project World Evacuation,"* the late contactee, Tuella, lays out in exquisite detail another take on what the Second Coming will include: the promise that some UFOs will assist in the "great exodus" of human souls off this planet. Tuella channeled Ashtar, her name for the alien Space Brother who "spoke" to her and other fellow believers. "You will be hosted by us, fed and housed comfortably in a great mother ship," Ashtar told her. Another Space Brother entity, called Andromeda Rex, even volunteered information about the food: "It will be as nearly normal to your accustomed foods as we can arrange it. It will include some drinks and foods that are new to you, but we are attempting a cuisine that will be favorable to all, with personal choices where needed."

It is comforting to know that the Chosen Ones will be well-fed in outer space, but the most joyous aspect of the great adventure will be "in the mingling of beings from all worlds," when the evacuated earthlings will be introduced to their galaxy and universe.

The exact time of the great evacuation is not known of course, but is contingent on events on Earth. For example, one message given in "Project World Evacuation" declares that, "We will not allow the entire planet to be destroyed. If atomic warfare does become activated, that will be the point of immediate mass evacuation by us of the prepared citizens of the Earth."

Tuella knows her audience. She is not preaching to the masses but rather to a specialized group prepared to understand her.

Before her passing, channeler Tuella was the primary represenative of the Ashtar Command.

"Just as many are called but few are chosen," Tuella writes, "likewise, many who read this book will neither understand nor receive the information. But those special souls for whom it is intended will rejoice in its guidance and accept its timely and imperative revelation.

"This information is not entertainment," she continues. "It is comparable to 'sealed orders' given to dedicated volunteers on a strategic mission. It is dispersed to them, compiled for them and will be cherished by them. It is neither defended nor justified. It is data recorded as given and passed on to those for whom it is intended."

There is a vaguely militaristic overtone to some of that passage; the phrases like "sealed orders" and "strategic mission" seem to imply that the Ashtar Command speaking through Tuella is extremely well organized and is definitely playing for keeps. But when you're talking about the rescue and salvation of yourself and your loved ones, who would have it otherwise?

It is unfortunate that Tuella passed away before she could be interviewed for this book because her input would have been fascinating. Her Space Brother contacts have given her a beautiful blueprint for an alien Rapture complete with information on the living arrangements onboard the ships afterward. As a race, we stand on the cusp of Doom and Salvation, and the mysterious, ubiquitous UFOs will be a crucial element of both.

UFOs will come in the middle of the night to take us away to a safe harbor in space should a global catastrophe be about to strike.

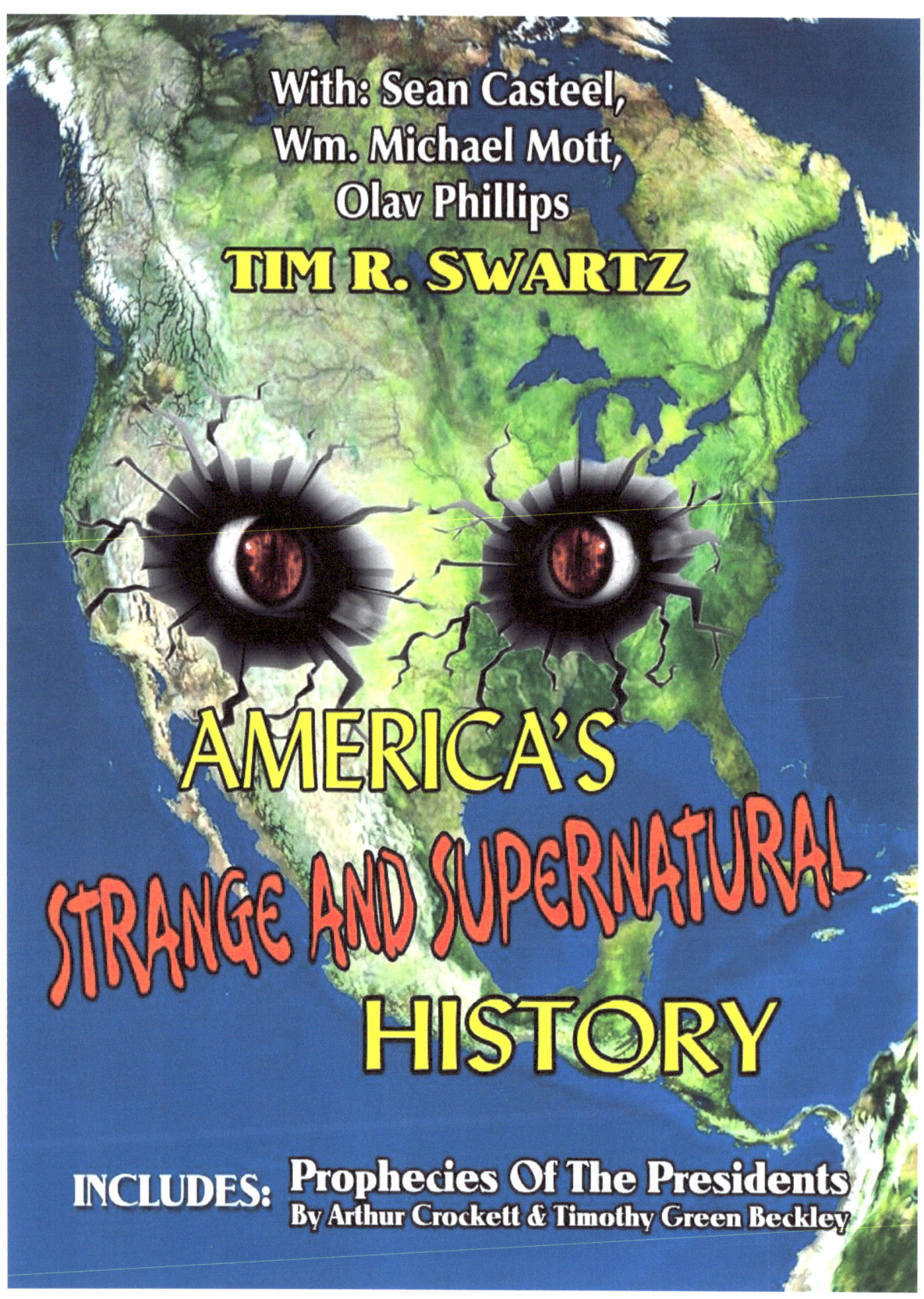

CHAPTER 5

America's Spiritual Destiny – From UFOs to the Prophecies of the Presidents

By Sean Casteel

Tim R. Swartz's book from Tim Beckley's Inner Light/Global Communications publishing house, "*America's Strange and Supernatural History*," recounts numerous little known paranormal and simply weird moments in the life of this nation. Everything from the "survival cannibalism" that took place in the American colony of Jamestown, to the mid-20th century crime spree of a disgruntled chemistry student, dubbed the "Mad Gasser," who used an aerosol anesthetic as a weapon, to the 18th century werewolf-type transformations of those foolish enough to have broken Lent seven years in a row in the French enclave of Vincennes, Indiana, are part of the heritage of the United States.

The bulk of the first section of "*America's Strange and Supernatural History*" includes the contributions of Wm. Michael Mott, Olav Phillips, Tim Beckley and, in the interest of full disclosure, myself. It is the second section of the new release that concerns us here: a reprint of the rare – but often referred to – "*Prophecies of the Presidents: The Spiritual Destiny of America Revealed*" by the aforementioned Tim Beckley and his late coauthor, Arthur Crockett. The authors make us aware that not only did our former presidents have contacts with the divine; they were also cognizant of their predestined place in history and readily accepted guidance and help from above.

PRESIDENTIAL UFO CONTACT

The presidents have also had their share of UFO contact along with matters more directly occult. The fact that Jimmy Carter saw a UFO in October 1969 and stated so publicly in 1973 is generally known among UFO enthusiasts, as is Carter's unfulfilled campaign promise to unlock the government's secret files and open the subject to public scrutiny.

However, *"Prophecies of the Presidents"* actually reprints the official report that Carter filed with the now-defunct National Investigations Committee on Aerial Phenomena (NICAP) as well as quoting comments from Carter's press secretary, Jody Powell, who told reporters: "I remember Jimmy saying that he did in fact see a strange light, or object, at night in the sky which did not appear to be a star or plane or anything he could explain. If that's your definition of an unidentified flying object, then I suppose that's correct. I don't think it's had any great impact on him one way or the other. I would venture to say that he probably has seen stranger and more unexplainable things than that during his time in government."

Jimmy Carter's UFO report to NICAP.

UFO SPIN DOCTORS

Perhaps less well known is the story of President Dwight D. Eisenhower's meeting with beings from outer space said to have taken place on February 20, 1954. Beckley and Crockett say the story has been confirmed for them by a member of the British Parliament of their acquaintance, among others. Eisenhower was vacationing in Palm Springs when he was summoned to Murdoc Airfield by high-ranking military officials. Murdoc was later renamed Edwards Air Force Base and served as the landing field for the space shuttle. Eisenhower canceled a scheduled news conference to go to Murdoc with the official explanation being that he was at the dentist.

Eisenhower and a handful of U.S. officials watched as five alien craft landed and the aliens disembarked, appearing something like humans but by our standards "misshapen." The aliens asked Eisenhower to begin a public education program about them for the American people and eventually the entire Earth. Eisenhower allegedly replied that the world was not ready for such an announcement and the aliens agreed to contact only isolated individuals until the people of Earth got used to the idea of their presence.

After demonstrating some of the capabilities of their spacecraft – and making the entire presidential contingent quite nervous by showing that they could become invisible at will – the aliens boarded their ship and departed. It is a generally accepted theory that we are currently experiencing a cultural conditioning program intended to help us gradually accept the fact that aliens are real and already among us, as the aliens requested that day at Murdoc.

Although Robert F. Kennedy never became president, he was a politician with enormous clout and influence whose political star was very much in the ascendancy when he was assassinated in 1968. The reader may not be aware that he had a definite belief in UFOs. In a personal letter to publisher Gray Barker of the Saucerian Press, Kennedy noted that he was a card carrying member of the Amalgamated Flying Saucers Club of America and indicated that he accepted the stories of those who claimed to have encountered aliens from other planets.

Kennedy wrote: "Like many other people in our country, I am interested in the UFO phenomenon. I watch with great interest all reports of Unidentified Flying Objects and I hope someday we will know more about this intriguing subject. Dr. Harlow Shapely, the prominent astronomer, has stated that there is a probability that there is life in the universe. I favor more research regarding this matter and I hope that, once and for all, we can determine the true facts about flying saucers."

UFO SPIN DOCTORS

Has the United States been assisted by extraterrestrial intelligence from the very beginning? - Art by Carol Rodriguez

What is important about stories like these, especially the Carter and RFK stories, is that they place the UFO phenomenon in a real-world setting where our leaders grapple with the unknown the same way we do and also burn with a curiosity they long to see satisfied. We are comforted that UFOs are not just a fixation of the fringe elements of society but are of genuine concern to even our most highly placed officials.

FIRST THINGS FIRST

Before that fascinating sojourn into presidential UFO lore, Beckley and Crockett begin by declaring that America has an important role to play in the coming New Age, what the authors call "an age of reason and enlightenment which is soon to engulf the entire planet we live on." Nothing in human history happens by chance, they believe, and so God intended the U.S. to help lead the entire world in the direction of freedom, love and perfect balance for all mankind.

"There is every reason," the authors write, "to believe that many of our Founding Fathers were reincarnated philosophers from Greece and Rome (and perhaps other planets) who originally lived in the time of Atlantis and had reentered physical shells in order to help reshape the history of the planet for centuries to come. Their main objective was to steer humans on the proper course and to see that this great nation got off on the right foot."

Reading this for the first time, I was struck by what an ingenious combination of various ancient spiritual ideas this concept was. When the authors speak of the Founding Fathers voluntarily being reincarnated to the physical plane to help guide America's birth, one is reminded of the Buddhist concept of the Bodhisattva, enlightened spirits who forego nirvana and willingly incarnate to happily share in the miseries of the world. Meanwhile, the authors' belief that our leaders are not selected by mere chance recalls the words of Saint Paul from the book of Romans, Chapter 13:1: "Let every person be subject to the governing authorities. For there is no authority except from God, and those that exist have been instituted by God."

GEORGE WASHINGTON'S VISIONS OF FUTURE AMERICA

Having mixed for us this heady cocktail of spiritual optimism and patriotic fervor, the authors next tell the story of George Washington, whom they say was supernaturally implanted with an indomitable faith in this country that saw him through the darkest parts of the Revolutionary War. Later in his life, Washington wrote a letter to the governor of Connecticut in which he stated that it was "almost possible to trace the finger of Divine Providence through those dark and mysterious days which led the colonists to assemble in convention, thereby laying the foundation for prosperity when we had too much reason to fear that misery and confusion were coming too rapidly upon us."

There had been moments in the war when Washington could be seen to openly weep, especially during the difficult winter of 1777, when his forces had suffered severe reverses on the battlefield and were close to starvation and freezing to death. He made a daily habit of going into a thicket, out of sight of his troops, to drop to his knees in prayer and ask for aid and comfort from God.

One day Washington gave strict orders that he not be disturbed in his headquarters so that he could draft an important dispatch without interruption. At one point he looked up and was startled to see a lovely young woman standing before him. She was by far the most beautiful creature he had ever seen, yet she had violated his privacy, so he asked her why she was there. After he had repeated the question four times, with no reply, he began to feel strange sensations and found himself unable to rise to his feet in the normal way of a gentleman greeting a lady. The room began to glow and Washington wondered if he was now dying.

George Washington told of an angel who revealed a prophetic vision of America to him at Valley Forge.

Finally, the woman raised her arm to the east and said, "Son of the Republic, look and learn." There followed a series of visions in which Washington was shown that the American nation would one day spread from the Atlantic to the Pacific Ocean. Another vision seemed to forewarn Washington about the Civil War to be fought less than a century hence. A third vision prophesied an invasion of America by the combined forces of Europe, Asia and Africa, which the authors link to the book of Revelation, Chapter 9:13-16. Those verses speak of troops that will be 200 million in number and wage war in the Last Days. Washington's visions concluded with the promise that America will emerge victorious from that future conflict and that her union will stand as long as there are stars in the sky.

WASHINGTON APPEARS IN A VISION TO GUIDE THE UNION

Washington is said to have appeared in a vision to Union General George B. McClellan at a point in the Civil War when the prospects for a northern victory seemed bleak. Washington warned McClellan that Confederate troops were set to descend on the nation's capital and score a decisive victory.

"General McClellan," Washington's voice spoke with amazing clarity, "do you sleep at your post? Rouse you, or ere it can be prevented, the foe will be in Washington! You have been betrayed, and, had God not willed it otherwise, ere the sun of tomorrow had set, the Confederate flag would wave above the Capital and your own grave. But note what you see. Your time is short."

As Washington spoke, McClellan beheld a "living map" which showed all the various troop positions. He took up a pen and copied down everything he saw. When Washington was assured that McClellan understood the military situation, he then spoke to the general about the 20th century, when other perils would beset the country even as America took its place as a leader among the nations of the world. McClellan would later write that the country would become "a Messenger of Succor and Peace from the Great Ruler, who has all nations in his keeping."

THE PRESIDENTS DENOUNCE ECONOMIC INEQUALITY

But not all the messages from the next world are so cheery and hopeful. *"The Prophecies of the Presidents"* also deals with information obtained through 19th century mediums like Lucy Brown, quite renowned in her day. She, too, felt she was in contact with the spirit of George Washington, who "predicted fascist dictatorship and its threat to America's destiny," according to Beckley and Crockett.

Union General George B. McClellan claimed that George Washington appeared to him in a dream.

"Clouds in the horizon that are looming up to overcast the future of America," Washington allegedly spoke through Brown, "becoming very dense, dark and foreboding ill, will burst in an unexpected moment upon the heads of her people. The mutterings of discontent, engendered by a sort of incipient, despotic rule, mild, perhaps, at present in its hold over the masses, and swelling into vaster proportions and power, is breeding discontent and disharmonies in the ranks of all classes of minds who labor diligently for a subsistence and gain a small and inadequate pittance of their hourly needs and daily bread."

This economic unrest among the working classes is due to the "widespread and desolating schemes of the robbers of the people of their rightful inheritance to life, land, home and pursuit of happiness." This financial chicanery does not go unnoticed by the hosts of spirits who dwell above the mortal sphere and can see into the secret workings of the minds and motives of the oppressors.

After Washington spoke, Thomas Jefferson added to the indictment by saying, "If the American people ever allow the banks to control the issue of currency, first by inflation and then by deflation, the banks and corporations that will grow up around them will deprive the people of all their property until their children will wake up homeless on the continent their fathers conquered."

President James Madison spoke even more frankly: "We are free today, substantially, but the day will come when our republic will come to impossibility because its wealth will be concentrated in the hands of a few. When that day comes, then we must rely upon the wisdom of the best elements in the country to readjust the laws of the nation to the changed conditions."

Abraham Lincoln confessed that he trembled for the safety of future America because, "As a result of war, corporations have been enthroned and an era of corruption in high places will follow. The money power will endeavor to prolong its reign by working on the prejudices of the people until all the wealth is aggregated into a few hands and the public is destroyed."

It was presumably a later medium that channeled Woodrow Wilson, who grimly charged that, "The masters of the government of the United States are the combined capitalists and manufacturers of the United States. The government of the United States at present is a foster child of the special interests. It is not allowed to have a will of its own. The government, which was designed for the people, has gotten into the hands of bosses and their employers, the special interests. An invisible empire has been set up above the forms of democracy. America is not a place of which it can be said, as it used to be, that a man may choose his own calling and pursue it as far as his abilities enable him to pursue it. American industry is not free as it once was free; American enterprise is not free."

THEIR WORDS FROM BEYOND THE GRAVE FULFILLED

I have quoted this section of "*Prophecies of the Presidents*" so carefully and extensively because it strikes me as being genuinely prophetic. The spirit voices of this small grouping of American chief executives are addressing what would in fact become a major issue for dissent in this country, as expressed by the Occupy Wall Street movement that began in September 2011. The movement's unforgettable slogan, "We are the 99 Percent," neatly summarizes the present condition of social and economic inequality suffered by the American people that has resulted from the greed, corruption and undue influence of corporations on government.

In 2012 and 2014, the media uncovered proof that the FBI and the Department of Homeland Security had monitored Occupy Wall Street through its Joint Terrorism Task Force despite labeling it a peaceful movement. Declassified documents showed extensive surveillance and infiltration of OWS-related groups across the country. Perhaps the wary suspicion of the two law enforcement agencies was also fueled by corrupt corporations seeking to guard their financial empires from a change in the national temperament.

Whether or not the "messages" spoken through the mediums were truly sent from the departed souls of some of our late presidents, or even if Beckley and Crockett made them up from whole cloth, they were nevertheless FULFILLED. One should realize that *"Prophecies of the Presidents"* was initially published in 1992, a full 19 years before the Occupy Wall Street movement first entered New York's Zuccotti Park.

Someone somewhere did indeed see the future and managed to get it written down in Beckley and Crockett's book. Some unknown power wanted it etched in stone and on the record. To me, that's a little uncanny. But, given my many years of writing for Tim Beckley, I guess I shouldn't be too surprised. He has always seemed to occupy some kind of publishing netherworld unto himself where books like *"American's Strange and Supernatural History"* with its *"Prophecies of the Presidents"* bonus reprint just come with the territory.

CHAPTER 6

Contacting Aliens and Angels With Cipher and Symbols

By Sean Casteel

Tim Beckley, the CEO of Inner Light/Global Communications, has always had a healthy interest in helping his customers make their personal spiritual journey to some kind of positive, joyful outcome. While Beckley resists some of the more "preachy" literary paths to salvation, he does inject into the marketplace a goodly amount of information intended to firm up your faith that there are patient, heavenly forces reaching out to those who are open to them.

Not only do these heavenly force reach out to us, we are provided with a method of reaching out to them as well. Which is the subject of a recent release from Inner Light/Global Communications called "*Angel Spells: The Enochian Occult Workbook of Charms, Seals, Talismans and Ciphers.*"

Perhaps some explanation about what the word "Enochian" in the title means. It refers to an "angel summoning" system first developed by John Dee, the most respected scholar of his day, in the 1500s when Queen Elizabeth I ruled over England. Dee, working with a psychic partner named Edward Kelley, attempted to open communications with the angelic realm.

I learned from my initial research into Dee and Enochian magick that it is an astonishingly complicated subject, so I turned to an expert. Aaron Leitch is the author of several books in the field that attempt to make the study a little easier for the uninitiated. Leitch told me that in the apocryphal Book of Enoch the prophet Enoch is said to have communed with angels on a regular basis and even to have been taken up to heaven and given a tour of the place. The book was later rejected from the Biblical canon and it was impossible to find a copy anywhere after it had been outlawed by the early Church many centuries before Dee's time.

John Dee claimed he could speak with angels and read the future. But he was also admired as a brilliant scientist, doctor, astronomer, and mathematician.

But Dee knew about the legendary Book of Enoch. He wrote in his journals that if Enoch, Ezekiel, Daniel and all the other prophets old had gotten their wisdom directly from angelic sources, why couldn't he do the same? So he began to explore occultism, reading medieval Christian magickal texts such as "The Keys of Solomon" and other sources that instructed the practitioner on how to call down angels and command demons.

Dee and Kelley would eventually create their own system for summoning angels that fused together the Jewish mystical work, the Kabbalah, along with the then current trends in Christian mysticism. Dee never called his system "Enochian Magick," however. That label was later applied by historians in reference to Dee's dedicated interest in the prophet's long lost book. But Dee saw himself as a faithful Christian even though his religious practices might have seemed a bit strange to his average fellow believers.

Having summoned the angels, either as a vision in Kelley's scrying stone (a variation on the more familiar crystal ball) or as audible speaking voices, Dee would write in his journal whatever the angels imparted. The problem quickly arose, however, that something besides the Queen's English was needed to make the conversations more authentic, more meaningful. What was to Dee a completely unknown tongue (sometimes called "The Language of Eden" because it was believed to have first been spoken by Adam in the Garden) was revealed to him by his angels. The language came to be called "Enochian" because it was given to the world by Dee in the course of his work.

"*Angel Spells: The Enochian Occult Workbook of Charms, Seals, Talismans and Ciphers*" includes the complete Enochian Keys, which are the requisite invocations to be spoken to summon the angels in both their preferred Edenic language and in English. There are also guides to pronouncing the Enochian words should you wish to experiment with all this a little yourself. According to author Aaron Leitch, who has written a two-volume study and analysis of the language called "The Angelic Language," one can bypass a great many of the complicated rituals, mathematics and encrypted instructions along with the language and still have a satisfactory angelic contact experience.

DID ENOCH HAVE AN ALIEN ABDUCTION EXPERIENCE?

And where do aliens fit in all this? The Book of Enoch has long been thought to contain elements of a typical alien abduction experience. Enoch is roused from his sleep by two angels and taken aloft to tour heaven. He is given information on the workings of the cosmos and then returned to his home. There is a school of UFOlogy that equates the angels who abducted Enoch and Biblical stories like Elijah's journey to heaven aboard a fiery chariot with basic elements of the present day UFO phenomenon. Dee sought to contact the same beings who had so graciously kidnapped Enoch, and it is left to us to wonder if he succeeded.

"*Angel Spells*" also tells the story of the legendary occultist Aleister Crowley's experiments with the Enochian magick he had learned while a member of the Hermetic Order of the Golden Dawn, an occult society founded in London in 1888. After Crowley broke with the Order, he continued to refine what he was taught until it became his own system.

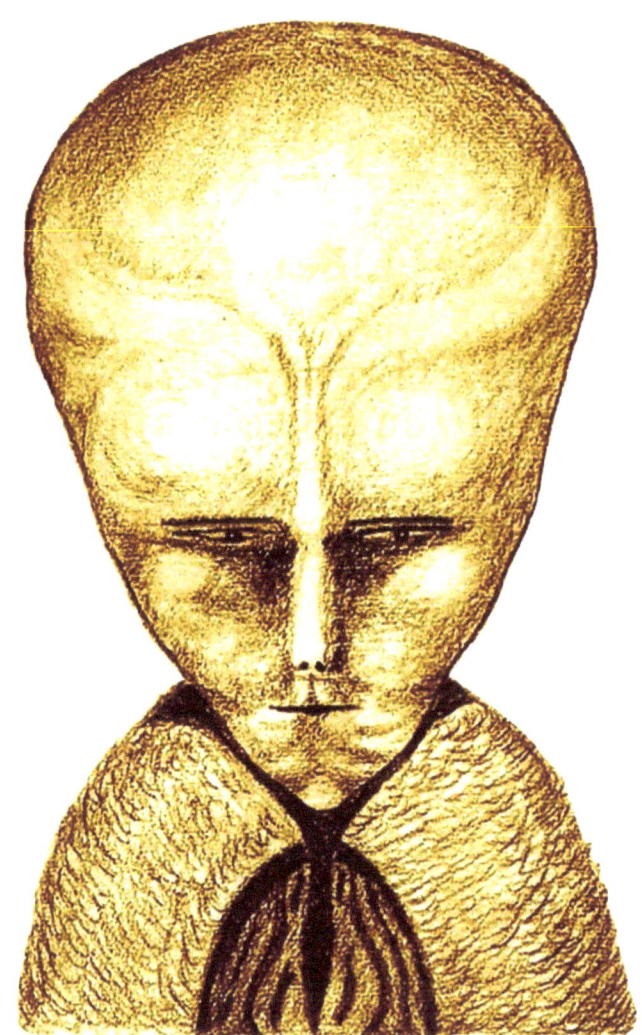

Aiwass is the name given to a voice that occultist Aleister Crowley reported to have heard in 1904. Crowley said that the voice dictated "The Book of the Law" (or Liber Legis) to him.

While on vacation with his wife in Cairo in April 1904, he received a surprising response to his many years of practicing Enochian magick: the appearance of "Aiwass," or "Aiwaz," a being Crowley regarded as super-human. The drawing that Crowley made in his journal at the time unmistakably resembles the familiar gray alien of our time. One is hard-pressed not to draw the conclusion that John Dee was most likely working with these same beings since he and Crowley were using such similar methods of summoning them. Crowley wrestled all his life with the nature of the Higher Beings he contacted, including Aiwass, and died in poverty in 1947.

SIMPLER RITUALS FOR CONTACTING ANGELS

The late William Alexander Oribello believed himself to be guided by angels from his childhood on and wrote several books for Tim Beckley that sought to teach others to do the same. Over the years, Oribello studied many sacred texts on communicating with the Angelic Kingdom. He discovered that there are certain times when they would be more readily available to come to our aid as well as offer guidance and support. Oribello always emphasized the importance of casting spells or praying while burning specific colored candles.

Oribello contributes a chapter to "Angel Spells" in which he summarizes his teachings regarding the Archangels, their influences, their association with various Zodiac signs and their relevance to specific days of the week. His chapter also features information about the type of candles to burn that will bring angels into our aura. He is able to make what could have been a strenuously complex cosmology into something charmingly simple and reassuring and even entertaining.

We are next given some female insight into all this by the Reverend Maria D'Andrea, an internationally known professional psychic from Budapest, Hungary. Maria gives simple step-by-step instructions on using some of Dee and Kelley's ritual objects and combining them with the angel symbols she created and which are included in her chapter. Maria follows that up with another chapter that teaches the reader to pray for safety and protection, how to use certain talismans and exactly which angel to summon for a specific purpose.

Here it is important to explain the "Workbook" part of the book's subtitle. Some of the ritual symbols in the book are intended to be photocopied onto cardstock or, preferably, virgin parchment. For example, there is a full-page reproduction of a symbol called the Sigillum Dei Aemaeth which was used by Dee in his Enochian rituals and is crucial to the magickal process. The idea is to photocopy the complex design and then use it as an altar in combination with the angelic symbols provided by Maria. This is all simpler than it might sound and does not require anything approaching the machinations of more pure forms of Enochian magick. One can also purchase the symbols already nicely printed out and thus avoid a trip to the photocopy store. Just check the ad in the back of "Angels Spells."

A special bonus section consisting of a reprint of Bishop Allen Greenfield's landmark book "Secret Cipher of the UFOnauts" is also part of "Angel Spells." Greenfield holds the title of bishop in the Gnostic Church and has a long history of active – and contentious – membership in many occult organizations, including the Ordo Templi Orientis, established by Aleister Crowley.

Greenfield's *Secret Cipher of the UFOnauts* is a provocative magickal text for the modern age that has come to be regarded as a classic in the field and one which might be considered to have a particularly hip cachet. For a long time it was a rare and difficult book to track down but it is included in full in "Angel Spells."

Allen Greenfield (right) is seen here with Timothy Green Beckley at the 32th annual UFO Conference. (Photo by Jim Moseley)

The book explains Greenfield's theory that much of the UFO phenomenon can be "decoded" by using a method that draws on the Kabbalah, especially the numerology aspects of its Jewish mysticism, as well as other similar ancient systems. He believes the UFO occupants are an eternal race that has always reached out to certain human adepts by using hidden, obscure linguistic and mathematical symbolism, including elements of Crowley's version of Enochian magick

THE ENDLESS POSSIBILITIES

Can contact with angels/aliens ever be something where we, as mere mortals, are an independent part of the conversation? Do we have the ability to bring such heavenly beings into our presence and then engage them in a dialogue in which they freely reveal what we are so eager to learn? Or does that sound a little too good to be true? Maybe you can answer that for yourself after reading "*Angel Spells: The Enochian Occult Workbook of Charms, Seals, Talismans and Ciphers*" and experimenting with some of the tools in the book.

However, be careful to approach all this with caution and to follow the instructions and rituals carefully. If you succeed in summoning an angel or two, you may find yourself in the company of something much more powerful than you ever imagined, an entity who is no respecter of persons and whose concerns and priorities are very different from your own. To quote Aaron Leitch, some of these angels can "fry your brain out with a single thought." But you may also experience ecstatic visions and draw inexpressibly nearer to God. The decision as to whether to take the risk is entirely your own.

Ancient Pre-Columbian Bearded Incense Burner with Semitic facial features found in Guatemala.

CHAPTER 7

"Pale Prophet" or Ancient Alien?
By Sean Casteel

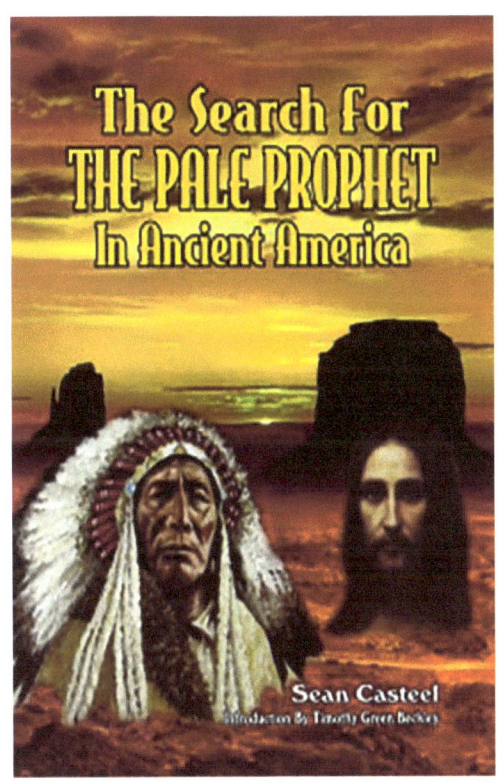

"The Search for the Pale Prophet in Ancient America."

The Pale Prophet who visited the Americas in the first century A.D. certainly knew how to make an entrance the people would never forget. And the full story is told in what I, as the author, believe to be an exciting new book titled "*The Search for the Pale Prophet in Ancient America,*" published by my associate Tim Beckley's Global Communications. Beckley is now co-hosting, along with Tim R. Swartz, the podcast "Exploring the Bizarre" on the KCOR Digital Radio Network.

According to ancient native lore, when the Fair God first arrived at the Polynesian Islands it was with three ships with giant sails like enormous birds with wings uplifted, glowing goldenly in the dawn light. The people watching the events were frozen to immobility.

"What manner of monsters are these with the great wings?" they asked in awe.

"Perhaps they have come to devour the people!" shouted one native.

Then the islanders saw something white moving toward them, apparently from the Great Birds. The white object glided easily over the water "with the rhythmical ease of a man walking."

"As the spot of white came closer," writes anthropologist L. Taylor Hansen, "they saw in amazement that this was a Fair God, manlike in form but unlike their people. Soon they could see Him clearly, the gold of the dawn light shining around Him, making a halo of His long curling hair and beard. As He came up on the wet sand, the warriors stared in fright at His garments; they were dry. Now they knew that a god stood among them, for none but gods can walk on water!"

Have aliens been hiding among us since the beginning of recorded history?

Putting aside for the time being the idea that we're dealing here with Jesus Christ himself, again displaying his ability to walk on water as recorded in the Christian Gospels, what we have here is a classic example of the "ancient astronauts" approach to the flying saucer mystery. A relatively primitive indigenous culture is confronted with what may be technological marvels that the natives ascribe to "gods" with abilities far beyond their comprehension. The ships with sails like huge birds with wings uplifted, for one, may be an attempt to describe a kind of flying craft that wasn't some form of a "boat" at all.

But none of the great "ancient astronauts" researchers, from Erich von Daniken to Zechariah Sitchin to Brinsley LePoer Trench, have ever covered the same territory as the late anthropologist L. Taylor Hansen, who spent decades traveling among the Native-Americans and collecting their legends regarding the Healer, the Prophet, the Miracle Worker, God of the Dawn Light, the Wind God, the Teacher, the White-Robed Master. Although the names are different, the legends are chanted and sung the same.

Very little is known about L. Taylor Hansen, who died in 1976. One thing that is known, however, is that her first name was Lucile, which she shortened to "L" so that she could pass herself off as a man, at least in literary terms. In 1918, while still a college student, she spent her summer vacation with the Chippewa Indian tribe in Michigan. According to writer Bette Stockbauer, who provides some of the scant biographical material available on Hansen, this interest was more than scholarly. The Chippewa's language and dances, their culture and religion, struck a richly harmonic chord in Hansen's soul.

Dark Thunder, the Chippewa chief, shared with young Hansen much of the tribal knowledge and told her of a Holy Man who had visited the tribe in long ago times. This man came to the Native Americans when their empire was united and their great cities stretched for miles. Wherever the Holy Man went, the miracles followed, and always He spoke of the Kingdom of His Father.

"In this brief story," Stockbauer writes, "Hansen sensed the germ of one much greater. That summer, a council of many tribes was called to tell the young lady the holy legends. Her own gift to the council would be a book that would preserve their words for future seekers. Thus was born '*He Walked the Americas*,' a book pursued over two continents, during the course of 45 years."

At the Indian council meeting, Hansen was charged with the mission of recording the legends of the Pale Prophet for posterity. But in the meantime, in order to meet her expenses, she sold science fiction stories to pulp magazines,

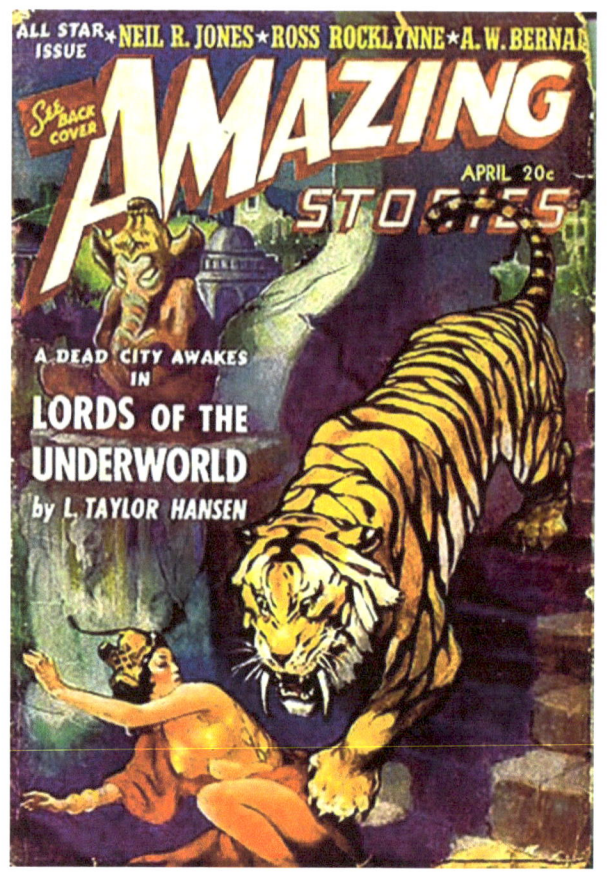

disguising herself as a man so she could succeed in a field completely dominated by the male element. In the 1940s, she was given space for a regular column in "*Amazing Stories*," a sci-fi pulp magazine, to air her nonfiction views on the current state of anthropology and archaeology. Ray Palmer, the magazine's legendary editor, not only published her "Scientific Mysteries" columns; he would also eventually publish "*He Walked the Americas*" in 1963 through his Amherst Press company and thus is an important figure in the overall story as well.

All of the foregoing is contained in "*The Search for the Pale Prophet in Ancient America*." In the first section of the book, I summarize and quote from Hansen's "He Walked the Americas" as well as adding my own Biblical insights and correlations not present in the original text of Hansen's groundbreaking work.

I think perhaps Hansen felt she was writing for the more "Biblically-literate" audience of her own time, or maybe she felt that the Biblical correlations were so obvious that they didn't need to be spelled out for the reader. In any case, I DID spell them out, and I hope it makes understanding the legends of the Pale Prophet a little easier. The more overt relationship of the legends to the Gospels will be dealt with in a separate article.

TRIBAL MEMORIES OF FLYING SAUCERS

Let us now return to the "ancient astronauts" view and the aforementioned essays by Hansen. In a piece called "Tribal Memories of the Flying Saucers," reprinted in full in the new Global Communications release, Hansen disguises herself as a Navaho Indian named Oga-Make. But the style of the writing is unmistakably her own even as she hides behind one of her known pen names, an identity that is again male along with being a pseudonymous Native American. This is the price she had to pay in the pre-feminist years of the late 1940s, when the essay was originally published.

"Most of you reading this," the essay begins, "are probably white men of a blood only a century or two out of Europe. You speak in your papers of the Flying Saucers or Mystery Ships as something new and strangely typical of the twentieth century. How could you but think otherwise? Yet if you had red skin, and were of a blood which had been born and bred of the land for untold thousands of years, you would know this is not true.

"You would know," the essay continues, "that your ancestors, living in these mountains and upon these prairies for numberless generations, had seen the ships before and had passed down the story in the legends which are the unwritten history of your people. You do not believe? Well, after all, why should you? But knowing your scornful unbelief, the storytellers of my people have closed their lips in bitterness against the outward flow of this knowledge.

"Yet, I have said to the storytellers this: now that the ships are being seen again, is it wise that we, the elder race, keep our knowledge to ourselves? Thus, for me, an American Indian, some of the sages among my people have talked, and if you care to, I shall permit you to sit down with us and listen."

Oga-Make/Hansen then shifts to a dialogue with the aged chief of the Paiute tribe.

The chief begins by saying: "You ask me if we had heard of the great silver airships in the days before the white man brought his wagons into the land. We, the Paiute nation, have known of these ships for untold generations. We also believe that we know something of the people who fly them. They are called The Hav-musuvs."

The flying saucer occupants, the Hav-musuvs, first came to the area in large rowing ships before the land became a dry desert. After the waters dried and the rowing ships were no longer of use to them, they created "flying canoes," which grew to become large silver ships with wings. The Have-musuvs built a city in the nearby caverns, where they dwelt in peace and were far removed from the bloody warfare of the other local violently combative tribes.

"Have you ever seen a Hav-musuv?" Oga-Make/Hansen asked.

"No, but we have many stories of them," the chief replied. "There are reasons why one does not become too curious. These strange people have weapons. One is a small tube which stuns one with a prickly feeling like a rain of cactus needles. One cannot move for hours, and during this time the mysterious ones vanish up the cliffs. The other weapon is deadly. It is a long silvery tube. When this is pointed at you, death follows immediately."

The chief described the appearance of the Hav-musuvs.

"They are a beautiful people," he said. "Their skin is a golden tint, and a headband holds back their long dark hair. They dress always in a white fine-spun garment which wraps around them and is draped upon one shoulder. Pale sandals are worn upon their feet."

The chief tells a fascinating legend said to have happened many years before the coming of the Spanish. A Paiute chief lost his bride to sudden death. In his overwhelming grief, he went seeking the Hav-musuvs in order that they put him out of his misery with their deadly silver tube. As the mournful chief climbed the last mountain on his quest, one of the men in white appeared suddenly before him, brandishing the silver tube and motioning the chief back. The chief made signs that he wished to die and continued onward. Then others of the Hav-musuvs appeared and decided to take the chief with them.

Many weeks after his people had mourned him for dead; the Paiute chief came back to his camp. He had been in the giant underground valley of the Has-musuvs, he said, where white lights which burn day and night and never go out, or need any fuel, lit an ancient city of marble beauty. There he learned the language and history of the mysterious people, giving them in turn the language and legends of the Paiutes. He would have been content to stay among them forever in the peace and beauty of their life, but they bade him return and use his new knowledge for the people.

Oga-Make/Hansen then asks the current Paiute chief if he believed the story.

"I do not know," the old man replied. "When a man is lost in Tomesha [a particularly forbidding stretch of hostile desert], and the Fire-God is walking across the salt crust, strange dreams, like clouds, fog through his mind. No man can breathe the hot breath of the Fire-God and long remain sane. This has always been a land of mystery. Nothing can change that. I must still answer your question with doubt in my mind, for we speak of a weird land. White man does not yet know it as well as the Paiutes, and we have ever held it in awe. It is still the forbidden 'Tomesha – Land of the Flaming Earth.'"

The short essay by Oga-Make/Hansen wonderfully embodies much classic "ancient astronauts" lore as well as timeless legends of a paradise hidden within the earth, which was also spoken of by the Tibetan seer T. Lobsang Rampa and many others. (Global Communications offers several of Rampa's titles to those seeking further enlightenment on the universal legends of Shangri-La.)

In any case, *"The Search for the Pale Prophet in Ancient America"* opens the reader to a whole new treasure trove of possible alien visitations to a land and a people long thought of as backward and savage. The Lord of Wind and Water and his civilizing influence on Native America is echoed not only in the Gospels but in the stories of ancient Sumer, Egypt and Babylon, who had uniformly credited gods from the sky with the beginnings of their organized societies. That that same helping hand also came to the ancient Americas, while generally acknowledged to be true, has never been told in quite the same way as it has by L. Taylor Hansen in *"The Search for the Pale Prophet in Ancient America."*

Original cover of "He Walked the Americas" published by Amherst Press.

CHAPTER 8

The Lore of Haunted Treasure and Connection with UFOs

By Timothy Green Beckley

Somewhere along the twisting path of the paranormal I discovered that UFOs and ghosts seemed to be attracted to buried treasure – either to guard it or lead to its discovery. Both phenomena have supposedly led prospectors directly to the proverbial "mother-load" or hovered so damn near it as to be beyond mere coincidence. I guess you could say they functioned as a sort of sign as to where to dig or dive – if the ultimate prize is underwater. Other times you better get your pistol or pick axe ready to protect yourself from the walking dead, though, come to think of it, neither instrument can wound or kill something that has already turned to dust. So it's better to hope you're light on your feet and can hightail it a safe distance away.

I have no statistics on any of these paranormal declamations, but I've heard an assortment of rumors. Now, in the case of UFOs, we're not talking about spaceships with humanoid pilots on board, but more likely ornery spook or ghost lights that seem to be under "intelligent control" but not piloted by "aliens" as we've come to imagine them – at least that is what I would assume.

Though I must say that one scribe pointed out to me that if the ancient astronauts known as the Annunaki were really coming here from Planet X thousands of years ago to take human slaves in order to mine for gold, perhaps they are still searching for this valuable substance – or perchance the slaves themselves are returning from the realm of spirits to haunt these particular locales as a form of retribution to their slave owners. It's all assuredly conjecture…pure speculation. But something uncommonly bizarre does seem to be going on that connects some lost treasures with the eerie sector of the phantasmal.

In all honesty, I first started to put two and two together "treasure-wise" and to think about any possible connection with the supernatural (the supernatural would include UFOs, which I believe to be more psychic in natural than physical hardware from outer space) when I started working out of Jim W. Moseley's office in Manhattan. Jim was the editor/publisher of "Saucer News," a magazine devoted to the investigation of unidentified flying objects. Jim was a well-known media personality, pushing subscriptions on TV and radio shows like the popular Long John Nebel Party Line, a five-hour talk fest that was broadcast nightly over WOR, a station that pumped out wattage over thirty states, creating a huge audience in the tens of thousands.

Spirits of pirates sometimes guard their buried treasures, while other times they may lead a sober, deserving individual to their troves. (Inspired art by Carol Ann Rodriguez).

UFO SPIN DOCTORS

Moseley had taken over my less-polished mimeographed zine – known as "The Interplanetary News Service Report" – and hired me as managing editor of his illustrious rag. JWM had garnered a somewhat "mysterious – lone wolf – reputation" among certain incredulous types in the UFO field who accused him of being a government agent or a member of some global cabal they loosely referred to as the "International Bankers."

One of the reasons for this negative notoriety seems to have been Jim's ability to disappear for considerable periods of time, leaving behind his Fort Lee, New Jersey, digs (he actually resided in Guttenberg, the next town over but picked up his mail from the same Post Office Box in Fort Lee for decades) and traveling overseas. Since his father had been in the military, this made him a prime contender for being a possible agent of darkness.

Truth is…Moseley and his father – U.S. Army Major General George Van Horn Moseley – had not spoken in years because of their highly polarized political views. This included taking particular exception to his father's outspoken racist and anti-Semitic views, including his claims that America must "breed up" its own decaying population by copying Nazi eugenics practices and launching a program of "selective breeding, sterilization, the elimination of the unfit, and the elimination of those types which are inimical to the general welfare of the nation."

UFO sightings are very common in Peru. Allegedly, they are seen over locations where treasure in one form or another is said to be buried.

Some have accused Jimbo of being a "tomb raider" because some of the artifacts he dug up while on "saucer sabbatical" in Peru were indeed buried more or less "six feet under," which technically made him a grave robber. The treasures consisted of everything from pottery to beautiful gold burial masks that bought him a fabulous fortune once he bribed Peruvian authorities to smuggle the pieces out of their country and into the U.S. where such "foreign relics" were NOT considered to be contraband.

Flying saucer provocateur, and Moseley's friend, Curtis Collins, has summed up Jim's treasure hunting days thus:

"For the next several years, Moseley divided his time between the U.S., 'Saucer News' and Peru treasure hunts. Jim's absences were a mystery to the flying saucer fans and 'Saucer News' readers and the subject of much speculation. This helped fuel fanciful rumors that he was a saucer spy! Also, while in Peru, Jim found time for both some real saucer work and also some mischief."

I knew Moseley very well on a personal basis from having worked with him daily out of his "Saucer News" office on Fifth Avenue. When he wasn't "out of town" on mysterious business dealings, I also partied until the wee hours with him and our sometimes wild gang of "saucer kooks" and had many discussions with Jim, both sober and inebriated.

At this stage, I don't profess to recall the intimate details, not having written them down, but Jim was certainly familiar with the lore and legends of Peru as far as ghost legends and flying saucers went. He said his frequent guide, a fellow by the name of Robert Kennedy, had told him that the spirits of the departed often guarded the places where they had been buried with valuables. I don't think they were intentionally hoarding these treasures from their position in the spirit world, but I am certain they had no intentions of having others dig them up centuries after they had been placed in the ground. That's sacrilegious in anyone's book.

Many a tomb, both in Peru and elsewhere, has a longstanding curse associated with it – especially ones that involve something valuable being buried underground. That's one of the reasons no one has ever located the Lost Dutchman Mine tucked away in the Superstition Mountain Range of Arizona outside of the heat-baked city of Phoenix. It's said that the spirits of the local native Indians, as appointed guardians, prevent anyone from getting anywhere near the cave where all the valuables are buried. Many have died and disappeared there, and some have even been abducted by UFOs, but that's another story for another time.

Regarding his treasure-hunting days in Peru, Jim had mentioned to me that mysterious flashing lights were being seen fairly frequently at high altitudes all over this South American country and there was some thought that flying saucers might be creating this unexplained phenomenon. Others have said that there is so much purportedly lost treasure in the mountainous regions around Machu Picchu that you can't possibly separate potential treasure from the UFOs hovering and streaking across the sky.

My friend and crystal skull explorer Joshua Shapiro said he became interested in the area near Lake Titicaca, Peru, after reading a book by Brother Philip (aka George Hunt Williamson) called *"Secret of the Andes and the Golden Sun Disk of MU."* In his book, Brother Philip describes a secret brotherhood in this area who administers a special school for those on the spiritual path.

"Lake Titicaca is even higher than Cusco. The Lake itself is very large and there are many islands within it. The large Peruvian city which is on the shore is called Puno, and this is where one stays. I know many of you have seen the derbies the women wear in Peru (which they got from the British, when they were there) and this is the case in Puno. Some of the local people have villages on the reed islands, and, in our last trip, we were able to go on one of their reed boats, which were very sturdy and comfortable. I asked our navigator if he ever saw UFOs in this area, and he said it is a common thing. Many people claim they have seen UFOs come in and go out of the water. Another friend told me that Jacques Cousteau once went in a submarine there to see what is under the water and was so shocked by what he saw that he has never spoken about this. My tour guide said the local people believe the Golden Sun Disk of the Inca is buried here. I think of all the places in Peru I visited, I saw more UFO-type 'clouds' here than everywhere else. Also, all the islands in the lake have stone terrace structures everywhere. The question I asked myself is, where did they get all these stones?"

MORE UFO TREASURE TALES

Up around Mt Rainier in Washington State where Kenneth Arnold saw a string of nine crescent-shaped UFOs back in June of 1947 there is so much gold said to be buried in them there hills that you need a state guidebook to plot them all out on a map. From time to time some happy go lucky prospector – yes there are still a few of the old breed still around laying claim to some secluded grubstake – will come into town carrying a pouch of sparkling nuggets, but it doesn't seem anything really to get excited about as the vast troves are still there for the taking if you happen to hit upon the right "ghost flame" to direct the way to the deep veins that exist below the earth, inside the mountain itself.

Actually, your best chance to come across a pocket of nuggets would be up around Yakima Indian Reservation,, though the locals certainly would not think highly of you if you absconded with what rightfully might be theirs according to tradition. At one point in the 1970s there were so many UFO sightings in the area that the Parks Department built a viewing stand from which the phenomena was even photographed.

Paranormal investigator Ryan Dube gives these additional details: "The Yakima Indian Reservation is located in the southern part of Washington state and covers roughly 3,500 square miles of both forest and flat land. The first reports were made by forest rangers in 1960, and most impressively Chief Fire Control Officer Bill Vogel reported a ninety-minute sighting of a mysterious ghost light in the sky over Toppenish Ridge. The officer reported that the light had a teardrop appearance (like a flame). Air Force investigators also became involved and gathered information on the light including photo and video footage. The lights attract both ghost enthusiasts and ghost hunters. Campers and Rangers observed and reported the greatest level of activity throughout the 1970s, and a number of witnesses even reported receiving telepathic messages from the lights as well as electrical devices failing."

Maybe this "natural" or supernatural phenomena persists because of the high concentration of certain minerals in the earth. I know from personal experience that a large crystal deposit can make any good spook light, as they are also called, jump to high heaven and attract a good deal of attention.

Fellow author and PSI proponent Preston Dennett says he has personally kept tabs on what has been called the Oriflamme Mountain Lights. "These light," Dennett insists, "have an ongoing reputation for hovering over areas where miners are known to have found gold and thus locally have become dubbed most appropriately 'Money Lights.'"

In his suspenseful book *"Supernatural California,"* Preston describes the Money Lights in rigorous detail.

"One famous location is the Oriflamme Mountain in the Southern California desert town of Anza-Borrego. Located on the western edge, the Oriflamme Mountain is composed of Granite and Schist bedrock. It has several streams which flow from it. Oriflamme Canyon is lined with oaks, sycamores, willow and cottonwoods. It is a popular site for hiking, camping and biking and remains a largely untouched wilderness area. The Oriflamme Mountain is also known for its mysterious ghost lights. The name "Oriflamme" actually translates as "Golden Flame." Apparently, the accounts of these lights reach so far back in history that the mountain was actually named for them. The lights occur all over the mountain and range out over the adjacent Borrego Valley desert.

"While the oral traditions are well-established for centuries, the first recorded account came in 1858, when a stagecoach driver passing by the mountain observed "phantom lights" dancing on the mountain. From that point on, reports began to pour in from other witnesses, including settlers, prospectors and soldiers.

"At first, the lights were thought to be from the spirits of the Native Americans who once inhabited the area. Several ancient Indian burial grounds are located in Oriflamme Canyon and the surrounding areas. True to their profession, however, prospectors generally theorized that the money lights, as they called them, indicated the presence of treasure or gold, and in fact gold has been found in the area.

Every year dozens search for the cursed gold of the Lost Dutchman's Mine - without success.

"One of the strangest and most famous of the sightings occurred in 1892, to a group of three prospectors camping near Grapevine Canyon. One of the men, Charles Knowles, described what happened. He and his companions suddenly observed three "lights" which looked like "fireworks" or balls of fire. The strange lights seemed to rise directly from the ground. They traveled in an arching pattern, reaching an elevation of about 100 feet. As they started to fall back down to the earth, the lights exploded. About thirty minutes later, the lights returned. On this occasion, the lights behaved very differently. They rose from the ground and arched up to 100 feet, but instead of exploding, they returned to the ground where they stopped, reversed in direction, and traveled back to their starting location. Clearly these are not normal lights!

87

"The sightings continued. Miners periodically saw the lights over the adjacent Vallecito Mountains and across the Borrego desert. At times, the lights reportedly lit up the night sky like a fireworks show. During the Prohibition era, it was speculated that the lights were caused by bootleggers. And at one point, the Oriflamme lights again came under suspicion for indicating the presence of illegal immigration or smuggling activities.

"Still, the lights continued to appear. Reports have continued on and off reaching to the present day. In the 1930s, a sighting of one of the mysterious ghost lights bobbing up and down along San Felipe Creek was reported to the American Society for Psychical Research, which printed the account in their journal. More recently, in October 2002, the International Earthlight Alliance (IEA) conducted a field investigation into the lights. The IEA is composed of scientists with various disciplines devoted to studying the phenomenon of earth lights.

"On October 18, 2002 Marsha Adams of the IEA headed a team of researchers for an on-site investigation. While the team did not observe the lights, they were able to interview firsthand eyewitnesses from the nearby town of Butterfield who confirmed that the lights still appear. Still, no explanation to account for earth lights has ever been found. One recent scientific theory is as bizarre as any other theory. It states that when strong winds blow sand up against large quartz outcroppings, they create a strong charge of static electricity. When the static-electric charge is strong enough, it discharges and causes the lights to flash. The area is now preserved as Anza-Borrego Desert State Park.

To reach Oriflamme Canyon, take Highway S-2 one mile south of the Box Canyon Historical site. There is a small sign that reads "Oriflamme Canyon." It is a three-mile dirt road that may require four-wheel drive. Stay left as the road forks and it will lead you to the base of the canyon. Here you will find some of the ancient Indian "morteros" or grave-sites. The canyon leads up to the south-west.

The mountain itself can be observed from Highway S2, four miles west of Butterfield ranch. Two dirt roads lead up to the mountain. The Butterfield Ranch Resort is located at: 14925 Gt. S. Overland, Julian, CA 92036. Phone: 760-765-2179"

I have been pleased to have Preston Dennett on as a guest on Exploring the Bizarre a weekly podcast I co-host with Emmy Award winning producer Tim R Swartz on the KCOR Digital Radio Network (all shows on archived at KCOR.Com or can be found on my YouTube channel "Mr UFOs Secret Files" – or simply under Tim Beckley. In the "golden days" of UFO newsstand publications

I relied on Preston to be a regular contributor to the now defunct "UFO Universe" and "UFO Files" magazines. I believe he told me last time we spoke that he had written seventeen books (don't hold me to that figure!) which included *"UFOs Over New Mexico,"* *"UFOs Over Arizona,"* and the forthcoming *"UFOs Over Colorado."* That's a hell of a lot of UFOs over somewhere.

Preston's conclusions. "UFOs definitely seem to be hovering over mines, and in some instances, are actively digging there in gold mines, silver mines, copper mines, uranium mines, you name it." Wild speculation? But certainly within the framework of this wondrous topic which hopefully will have you turning these pages till you have come to the end. You ARE invited to stop on over to Preston's website anytime – http://prestondennett.weebly.com

Exploring the Bizarre - With Timothy Green Beckley and Tim R. Swartz, Thursday nights at 10 PM Eastern (7 PM Pacific) on KCOR Radio. kcorradio.com

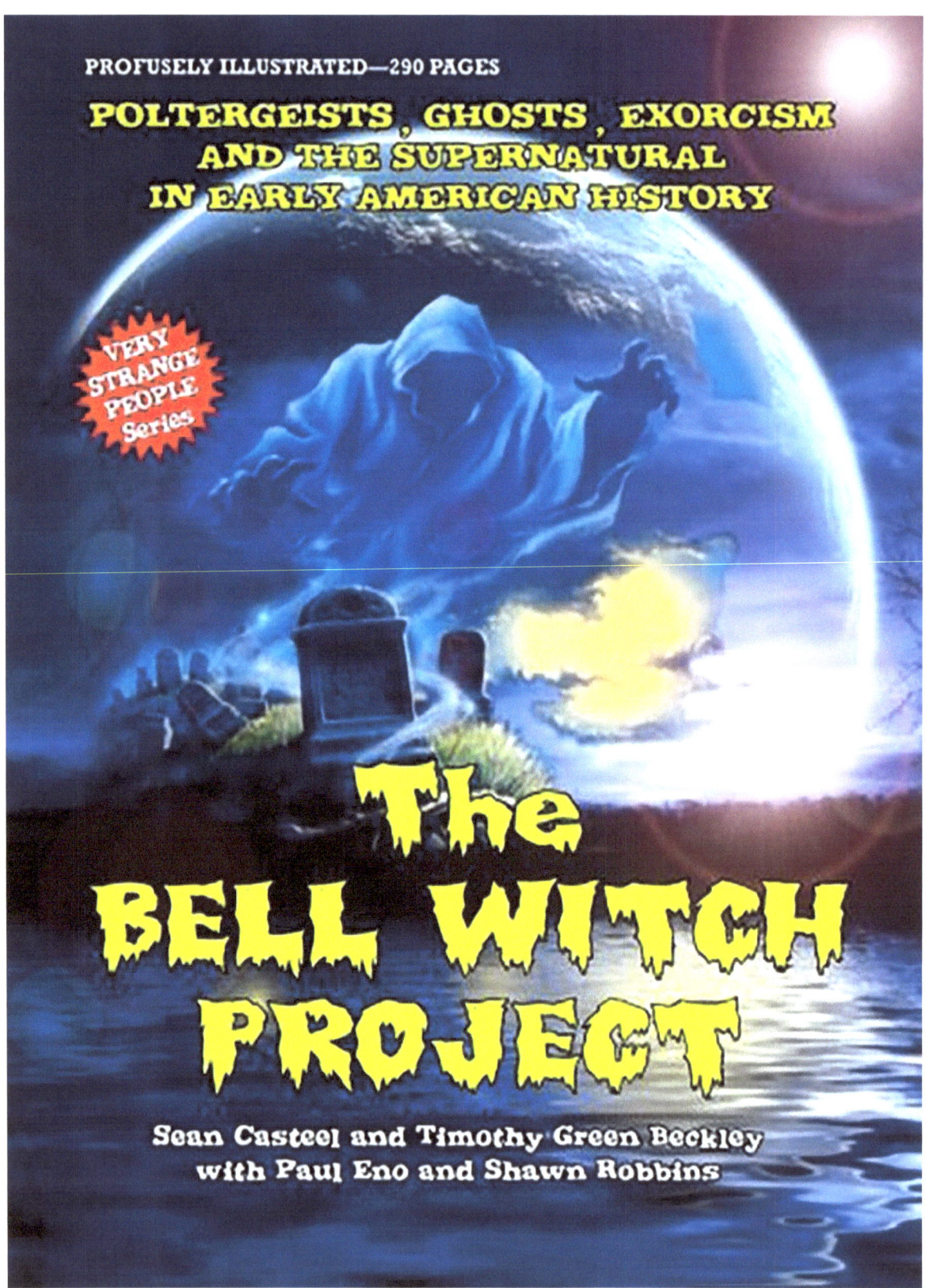

CHAPTER 9

The Murderous Mystery of the Bell Witch

By Timothy Green Beckley

New York, NY – Movie goers might have seen the various scary Hollywood horror versions of this terrifying early American ghost story...but until recently the chilling haunting and poltergeist case that transpired in rural Yalobusha County, Tennessee back in 1817 has never been properly examined or consequently explained. The full story is recounted in the newly released "*The Bell Witch Project: Poltergeists, Ghosts, Exorcism, and the Supernatural in Early American History*," co-written by Paul Eno and published by Inner Light/Global Communications.

Paul Eno is dead serious about investigating the paranormal.

Photo of the Bell House taken around 1909.

The Bell Witch Project details the story of the Bell family, who were subjected to a long and frightening siege at the hands of a "monster" that invaded their home. The haunting ultimately gained an international reputation that has lasted to this very day.

The events began when John Bell, a highly respected farmer in a rural community called Adams, was confronted by a strange dog-like creature that suddenly appeared out of nowhere and then vanished. There soon followed strange, unexplainable noises in the house, sounds like knocking on doors and windows, wings flapping against the roof and animals fighting and scratching. As the noises became more intense, the family tried desperately to find the source, but to avail. One night the spirit began to speak, introducing itself with hysterical, mocking laughter and calling itself "Kate."

From then on, Kate never ceased to speak, arguing theology, teasing, tormenting and spreading gossip. She seemed to know intimate details about everyone and took great delight in pestering the household at will. When asked why she had chosen to torment the Bell family, the spirit said she was a witch conjured by the late Kate Batts, an eccentric old woman who had placed a deathbed curse on John Bell for cheating her husband in a business deal some years before. Kate unleashed all hell on John Bell, throwing dishes and furniture at him as well as pulling his nose and yanking his hair. She yelled at night to keep him from sleeping and snatched the food from his mouth as he ate.

Andrew Jackson, the future president, had heard about the widely publicized witch and paid a visit to the Bell home to see for himself. He is said to have left the next morning saying he would rather fight the British in New Orleans than have to fight the Bell Witch. As for John Bell, after years of physical abuse from Kate, he died. His funeral was attended by hundreds of friends and curiosity seekers who could hear Kate laughing and mocking the family, even singing in her triumph.

But the eerie story of the Bell Witch is only a prelude to things even stranger. According to paranormal investigator Paul Eno, America has in general had a long history of fascination with the supernatural. For example, in the six New England states, in the years between 1770 and 1900, vampires were said to inhabit bodies of the dead and to prey only on members of their own families.

The witch was said to have appeared once to the Bell Children.

The grave of Mercy Brown who died from tuberculosis, but was thought by locals to be a vampire. When she was dug up, her body was in "pristine" condition. Her heart was removed and burned to stop her vampirism.

In one case, a father petitioned the town council for permission to dig up the body of his 23-year old daughter because she was rising from the grave each night to drain the lives of her eight brothers and sisters. It was believed the body of the vampire must be exhumed and the bones broken to prevent its moving about. Also, the heart must be burned and ailing family members might be aided by inhaling the smoke from the fire or eating the ashes.

Eno also writes about a possible early cause for the Salem witch hysteria in Massachusetts: the 1692 invasion of the nearby town of Cape Ann by what came to be called the Specter Leaguers, seemingly an army of ghosts or demons. The intruders were impervious to lead or steel and could show themselves first in one place, then in another. They threw stones and beat upon barns with clubs. These specters appeared both night and day, dressed in white and carrying "bright guns," though they acted more like hooligans than soldiers. Some feared an attack by the Indians, the French, or worse, while others believed it was an invasion by demons and that the Devil was loose in Cape Ann.

To round out the vampire and demon stories, Eno discusses a poltergeist incident that took place in Stratford, Connecticut, in 1850. A retired minister and his family were haunted by strange effigies, made from the family's clothing that appeared out of nowhere. Objects began to move around the house, with forks, spoons and knives being launched from places where no one was standing. The nighttime hours were filled with rapping, knockings, voices, screams and other bizarre sounds. By finally conducting a séance, the minister made contact with the poltergeist, who told the beleaguered reverend that it was a spirit in hell enduring torment for the sins it had committed in life. It said it had been troubling the minister's household "for fun."

And to think it all started with the Bell Witch and went on from there!

* * * * *

ABOUT PAUL ENO: One of the most dependable paranormal investigators, Paul Eno has had a distinguished career as a newspaper and magazine reporter and editor. He is the author of seven books including "*Footsteps In The Attic*," and "*Faces At The Window*," which are considered classics of the paranormal genre. Paul has appeared multiple times on "Coast To Coast AM" with Art Bell and George Noory, as well as appearing on the Travel, Discovery and History Channels. Paul's unusually long experience in the field (nearly 45 years), his hair-raising adventures with famous hauntings, along with his unique theories about the paranormal and its meaning for our understanding of the world and ourselves, make him a major draw on the talk show and lecture circuit. He co-hosts, along with his son, Ben, a weekly radio program called "Behind the Paranormal" that boasts an estimated three million listeners. Those wish to interview Mr Eno should contact him directly at:

paul@behindthebaranormal.com

To find out more about Paul Eno and his work, go to:

www.newenglandghosts.com

The website for his radio show is: www.behindtheparanormal.com

CHAPTER 10

The Dog-Awful Truth Behind "Cryptid Creatures"

By Sean Casteel

They are the demon dogs from hell, the huge black canines with blazing eyes that haunt country lanes, and the phantom hounds that are regarded by some as Satan's personal minions.

In the new Global Communications/Conspiracy Journal book, "*Timothy Green Beckley's Cryptid Creatures From Dark Domains: Dogmen, Devil Hounds, Phantom Canines and Real Werewolves,*" the reader will indeed discover that there exists on the periphery of UFOs and aliens a shadowy realm of supernatural phenomena that includes many weird crypto-zoological monsters and creatures, none of which are housebroken and do not in any way, shape or form, make good domestic pets . . . demon dogs or hellhounds included!

Encounters with the oversized, flaming-eyed canines of torment and terror have been reported through the ages and have often been associated with subsequent death or other forms of tragedy. To hear such a creature howling in the night is to tread close to danger of many kinds.

BUTCH WITKOWSKI STALKS THE DOGMAN

In an interview conducted exclusively for this book, Butch Witkowski talks about his research into what he calls a "bipedal canine" that is frequently reported to appear in the state game lands of central Pennsylvania.

Witkowski began to study the paranormal after a UFO sighting he shared with several people went completely unacknowledged and unreported by the government and media. After he set up his own organization, called the UFO Research Center of Pennsylvania, with a gathering of like-minded UFO-believing individuals, he was surprised by the increasingly numerous reports of a doglike creature walking on two legs that were coming into the group.

"This is a real mystery to me," Witkowski said. "You know, I thought Ufology was strange and hard to figure out, but it's kind of simple compared to this stuff."

The first report came to Witkowski in November of 2014 from a reliable witness – a retired pilot with 40 years of experience in both the military and with commercial airlines. Pilots are highly trained observers; it is a vital part of their job to accurately understand what their eyes behold. The pilot told Witkowski that he had been walking his two dogs in a familiar stretch of woods when the canines suddenly went berserk for no apparent reason. Next, the man beheld a tall, hairy, short-snouted "whatever the hell it was" that seemed totally oblivious to both him and his agitated hounds.

Chief investigator Butch Witkowski has heard from witnesses who say that when the creature appeared they feared for their lives.

The man described the creature to Witkowski by saying, "If you would take Arnold Schwarzenegger and make him eight to ten feet tall – same body, massive chest, very thin waist, heavy-legged, muscular arms with hands."

The man added that he didn't see any ears, but he remarked that he hadn't really looked for ears. He had taken in the whole creature, which had a short snout similar to a bulldog or pug.

After struggling to get his dogs back in his vehicle, the man pulled a handgun out of the glovebox and walked into the woods again. He saw nothing. No broken branches or footprints. The man subsequently returned to the scene – ignoring Witkowski's advice – with several heavily armed friends. Although the group saw nothing, they simultaneously began to feel deathly afraid, as though an invisible presence was making them fear for their lives. They literally walked backwards out of the area, too frightened to turn their backs on whatever was generating that collective terror.

Dogman is said to have the body of Arnold Schwarzenegger and the face of a fierce bulldog.

Another Pennsylvania resident, a woman raised in a religious family, told Witkowski about seeing a similar creature standing at the edge of a pond near her home. The woman had been taught that – if she were ever to see the devil – he would appear to her in animal form. "I truly believe," she told Witkowski, "that I was looking at the devil."

The creature is often called "demonic," according to Witkowski. He has also consulted Native Americans, including members of the Inuit and Cherokee tribes, who have told him they think it may be a creature called a "skin-walker," a shape-shifting spirit that could have gotten stuck somewhere between human and animal forms.

Whatever the creature is, it consistently terrifies those who encounter it.

"One thing that stands out in every report," Witkowski said, "is that the people feel 'This is not a good place to be right now. I need to get out of here or I'm going to die.' They have a fear that comes over them that just sets the impulse to fear and flee right into motion instantly, the minute they see it."

THE HOLLYWOOD HELLHOUND

Michele Lowe is a paranormal researcher who relates a fascinating personal experience in *"Cryptid Creatures From Dark Domains."*

"When I was in my late teens, early twenties," she writes, "I used to hang out with my friends, like most people in Southern California. But I was a little weird. I loved all things Hollywood. I would recruit my friends all the time to go with me up to Hollywood to hang out."

Lowe first recounts a few Hollywood ghost stories, like hauntings by "Superman" actor George Reeves and Paul Bern, the husband of blond bombshell actress Jean Harlow. Both Reeves and Bern committed suicide and their troubled spirits can find no rest. Along with cruising the streets where ghosts allegedly materialized on a regular basis, Lowe and her friends were curious about seeing the house at 10050 Cielo Drive, where the Manson family had murdered pregnant actress Sharon Tate and several of her friends and peers.

They had to drive up a steep and narrow driveway before reaching the home's iron gate, which was where the first body was discovered the morning after the killings in 1969.

"The feeling of being so close to where such a horrific crime was committed," she continues, "was very sobering. The atmosphere was very heavy there, and it just didn't feel right. So we left."

Lowe writes that they decided to explore some of the other Hollywood neighborhoods, consoled by the bright lights and a more cheerful ambience.

It was then that a giant black dog came charging at the car.

"It was huge," she recalled, "and had this very thick black fur. The dog's back and head easily came up to the window of the car."

Lowe and a female friend screamed in panic while Cuz Dave, the driver, hit the gas pedal. Even when the car reached 35 mph, the dog had no problem keeping up the pace.

"It was literally right next to the car," Lowe writes, "looking at us as if it was out to kill! It was barking violently as we tried to drive away in sheer terror. We drove about a mile or so before Dave finally slowed down and turned into another neighborhood so we could calm down and regroup. Just as we were starting to calm down, the giant black dog literally appeared out of nowhere and came charging at the car.

"We again screamed and Dave took off again. We could not believe this was happening. There was no way that dog could have kept up with us when Dave took off out of that last neighborhood over a mile away! We quickly got out of that neighborhood and again lost the crazed dog. This time, though, we didn't stop. We went straight home."

Many readers, according to Lowe, might mistakenly think the young people were only dealing with someone's pet. But she counters that assumption, saying she had never seen a dog so enormous. Its speed was also mind blowing, since it ran right next to the car without straining to keep up.

"It was clear the dog could have run even faster if it wanted to," Lowe writes. "And then there is the fact that we drove off as fast as we could a mile or more away to another neighborhood and were there only a couple of minutes when, literally out of nowhere, the dog appeared again and started charging us at full speed. How could it even find us again? Even though we didn't understand it then, we still knew that what happened was not normal."

Over the ensuing years, Lowe began to study the paranormal in a quest for answers to the brush with the supernatural she and her friends had shared.

It is known by different names...Hell Hound, Black Shuck, or the Black Dog. Either way, it has incited terror for centuries.

"Knowing what I know now," she reasons, "I believe that what we encountered was a hellhound. I had heard of them before but didn't know what they were. So I did some research and this is what I found: A hellhound is a supernatural dog, usually very large with thick black fur. They are unnaturally strong and fast and have red eyes. Sometimes the eyes are yellow. It is said that they are assigned to guard the entrance to the home of the dead, like graveyards or burial grounds. They also have other duties to do with the afterlife, like hunting down lost souls. They can also be an omen of death."

NICK REDFERN STRUGGLES WITH THE FIERY HOUNDS – AND A UFO CONNECTION!

"*Cryptid Creatures From Dark Domains*" also features the work of Nick Redfern, one of the most visible faces in the field of paranormal research. Redfern has testified that his bedroom was once "invaded" by a werewolf-type creature which crept closer and closer to where he was sleeping and then suddenly vanished. Redfern begins his chapter with a genuinely frightening story, told in second person, of a hapless traveler encountering a hellhound and fleeing for his life. One is then informed that the story was not a work of fiction, but actually happened in 1997 in a small English village called Ranton.

"But what are these infernal creatures?" Redfern asks. "Are they legend, reality, or both? And how, and under what circumstances, did they inspire the most famous, cherished and loved Sherlock Holmes story of all time? Published in 1902, Conan Doyle's *'The Hound of the Baskervilles'* tells the memorable and atmosphere-filled saga of the noted and wealthy Baskerville family that has called Dartmoor, Devonshire, England, its home for centuries. Dartmoor is filled with supernatural tales of terror, horror and intrigue – but leading them all is the legend of the terrible hound that haunts the Baskervilles."

Conan Doyle took the lead from all-too-real supernatural occurrences of the paranormal hound on Dartmoor. He also relied on stories about a real-life resident of Devonshire County named Richard Cabell, a monstrously evil squire who may have sold his soul to the Devil himself for personal gain. When Cabell died in 1677, presumably into the embrace of his fork-tailed, horned master, a pack of supernatural hounds materialized on the old moors and raced for Cabell's tomb, where they howled ominously all night long and struck cold fear into the locals.

"Thus, the story began to develop in Conan Doyle's mind and imagination," Redfern continues. "He moved the location of the old hall to Dartmoor and changed Richard Cabell to the evil Hugo Baskerville. In the process, literary history was made and *'The Hound of the Baskervilles'* was born. But there is one important factor to remember: Conan Doyle did not invent Britain's fiery-eyed hounds. He merely brought them to the attention of the public in spectacularly entertaining, fictional style."

For those looking for a possible link to the UFO phenomenon, one does not have to travel through a black hole to find what appears to be a very positive connection.

It is at this point that Redfern begins to chronicle several instances of people encountering the real thing, and in more recent times than one might think. For example, there is the story of Nigel Lea, who in the early weeks of 1972 was driving across the Cannock Chase woods that dominate much of Staffordshire when he saw a strange ball of glowing blue light that seemingly came out of nowhere and slammed violently into the ground some short distance ahead of him before releasing a torrent of bright, fiery sparks. As he slowly approached the area where the light had fallen, he was both shocked and horrified to see looming before him "the biggest bloody dog I have ever seen in my life."

In many instances, UFO hot spots have also become havens for the sightings of cryptids, including Bigfoot, Dogman and alien reptilians.

"Very muscular, and utterly black in color," Redfern goes on, "with a pair of large, pointed ears and huge thick paws, the creature seemed to positively ooze both extreme menace and overpowering negativity, and had a crazed, staring look in its yellow-tinged eyes. For 20 or 30 seconds, both man and beast alike squared off against each other in classic stalemate fashion, after which the animal both slowly and carefully headed for the darkness and the camouflage of the tall surrounding trees, not even once taking its penetrating eyes off of the petrified driver as it did so."

Somewhat ominously, two or three weeks later, a close friend of Lea's from back in his childhood days was killed in a horrific industrial accident in a West Midlands town. Today, after having deeply studied – almost to the point of obsession – the history of British Black Dog lore and the creature's associations with both deep tragedy and death, Lea believes his strange encounter was directly connected.

BLACK SHUCK AND THE SHUG MONKEY IN RENDLESHAM FOREST – AND, YES, YOU'VE HEARD OF THAT PLACE BEFORE!

According to Redfern, perhaps the most famous of all of the phantom hounds of old Britain are those that are said to have frequented, and in some cases still frequent, the ancient roads and pathways of Norfolk, Essex, Suffolk and Sussex. Their various names include Black Shuck, the Shug Monkey and the Shock. The Shuck and the Shock are classic black dogs, whereas the Shug Monkey is described as being a combination of spectral monkey and immense hound.

"Even their very names have intriguing origins," Redfern writes. "While some researchers consider the possibility that all of the appellations had their origins in the word 'Shucky,' an ancient east coast term meaning 'shaggy,' others suggest a far more sinister theory, namely that Shock, Shuck and Shug are all based upon the Anglo-Saxon 'scucca,' meaning 'demon,' a most apt description for sure."

In the winter of 1983, a couple in their twenties, Paul and Jayne Jennings, encountered a black dog in Rendlesham Forest, home to Britain's most famous UFO encounter, the December 1980 event in which numerous personnel from the nearby Royal Air Force Bentwaters military base encountered a UFO in the woods. Like Nigel Lea's witnessing a glowing blue light before his face-to-face meeting with a black dog, the close proximity of the military's UFO incident creates a tenuous connection between both phenomena. **Memo: Go to our Mr. UFO Secret Files YouTube channel for the exclusive story – https://www.youtube.com/watch?v=a8QScAUN-pE**

DOGMAN STRANGE MISTS AND FOGS APPEAR

The Jennings were walking along a trail in the Rendlesham Forest when, according to Redfern, they saw what Jayne described as a "big black dog that kept appearing and disappearing." When Redfern asked her to elaborate, she explained that on rounding a bend on the path they came face to face with the dog, which was a huge creature whose head was unmistakably that of a large hound while the body, strangely, was more feline in nature.

The dog was not aggressive, and seemed to have a mournful expression on its face. But the Jennings were shocked when it vanished in the blink of an eye. They were even more shocked when a moment later it reappeared and proceeded to "flicker on and off" four or five times before vanishing permanently. After the dog's disappearance, the air was filled with a strange smell that resembled "burning metal." Could it be the fires of hell, to which the mournful-looking dog was dispiritedly returning? And what of the possible Rendlesham connection? Are the weird goings-on there proof that this might be what John Keel once determined to be a "window area" to another dimension?

THE HOUNDS IN MYTHOLOGY

Further along in his chapter, Redfern tells the story of the Wild Hunt and even wilder hounds. He quotes the famed crypto-zoologist Jon Downes: "Belief in the Wild Hunt is found not only in Britain but also on the Continent, and the basic idea is the same in all variations: a phantasmal leader and his men accompanied by hounds who 'fly' through the night in pursuit of something. What they are pursuing is not clear; although Norse legend has various objects such as a visionary boar or wild horse, and even magical maidens known as Moss Maidens.

"Greek myth has Hecate roaming the Earth on moonless nights with a pack of ghostly, howling dogs and the phenomenon has also been reported from Germany, where, according to folklore, the procession includes the souls of unbaptized babies in the train of 'Frau Bertha,' who sometimes accompanied the wild huntsman."

(The mythic apparition of the Wild Hunt is said to resemble, and may have inspired, a well-known Country and Western song called "Riders in the Sky," in which a band of ghostly cowboys is condemned forever to chase a herd of cattle across the sky yet never actually catch them. The song has been recorded by the likes of Johnny Cash, Gene Autry, Bing Crosby and Peggy Lee, as well as a later rock version by The Outlaws.)

Downes explains that the hounds are universally believed to be portents of war, death and disaster, and an unfortunate traveler who heard one would fling himself face downward to the ground to avoid seeing the beast. The Devil's hunting packs, and the related phenomenon of the Devil Dogs, have been reported on more occasions during years of warfare than at any other time.

BLACK DOGS FROM COLONIAL TIMES TO THE PRESENT

"Legends of black dogs and phantom hounds," Gable writes, "are widespread throughout the Chesapeake Bay region, which was one of the earliest areas settled by the English. The tales of British black dogs were combined with werewolf traditions and typical ghost stories, as well as possibly with crypto-zoological sightings of weird creatures, to create traditions that are like the British ones, and yet unlike them at the same time."

One of the interesting stories Gable relates concerns a phantom hound named "Snarly Yow" who haunted a section of the National Pike near Turner's Gap in Frederick County, Maryland. Gable references an 1882 book by Madeleine

V. Dahlgren called "South Mountain Magic" in which no less than a dozen sightings of the beast are recorded.

A man named Daniel Mesick testified that his father kicked at a huge dog near Dame's Quarter and his foot passed directly through it. Sticks, rocks and even bullets were said to pass right through the "animal." Other accounts have it that the dog left physical traces and frightened horses so much they threw their riders.

"A staple of Frederick County legendry for years," Gable writes, "the Yow was seen in 1962 near Zittlestown. In this instance, it was headless, white and dragged a chain along behind it."

There is a phantom dog called the Fence Rail Dog, an enormous hound nearly ten feet long, which haunts a stretch of Route 12 near Frederica in Delaware. The dog appears in the wake of automobile accidents on the road. Gable points out that folklore from around the globe speaks of dogs as a kind of psycho-pomp – or spirits which guide the dead to the afterlife – and that the Fence Rail Dog's appearance in the wake of death may be an example of this.

Gable also recounts the folklore concerning an outlaw named Silas Werninger, who was cornered in his home but committed suicide rather than be taken by his pursuers. He was buried in the forest near his home, and after his death a large black wolf emerged from the grove and menaced townspeople. A witch advised the people to dig up the outlaw's remains and bury them in consecrated ground to dispel the phantasmal wolf.

Gable says the source of the folklore is the real life story of a Pennsylvania outlaw named William Etlinger, who did indeed kill himself after taking his wife and children hostage. His cabin was burnt to the ground by authorities trying to flush him out. It is said that the cabin sometimes reappears on its burnt foundations and that the outlaw's body was moved after it was felt a black wolf familiar in the area may have been feeding on the corpse. Even suicidal outlaws deserve better. There is more to the story Gable tells than is recorded here, but let's leave that to readers of the actual book, eh?

DEMON DOGS AND THE MIB?

Claudia Cunningham, nicknamed "The MIB Lady," relates the story of how she and Timothy Green Beckley visit the grave of Charles Fort in Albany Rural Cemetery, near the state capitol of New York. Cunningham says that perhaps the site where Fort and his entire family are entombed is a fitting place for dastardly black hounds and phantom dogs from hell to be seen since Fort collected such beastly stories throughout his writing career and placed them in the volumes that make up *"The Complete Works of Charles Fort."*

While Cunningham and Beckley failed to see any phantom dogs, their story still makes for a lively break in the action, to include some local Men-In-Black stories that center around the cemetery just outside Albany. In addition to being the place where Charles Fort is buried, the graveyard is the resting spot of a president of the United States, Chester Arthur. Is it any wonder haunting hounds, the MIB and other strange incidents raise their heads up from the etheric there from time to time?

Cunningham then goes on to record several late 19th and early 20th century stories from Fort's research concerning the mysterious slayers of sheep in the UK. In one case in England, the police were unable to explain how the sheep had died since it was not possible for the killer to have been a mere dog.

"Dogs are not vampires," said Sergeant Carter of the Gloucestershire Police, "and do not suck the blood of a sheep and leave the flesh almost untouched."

Tim Beckley and the MIB Lady, Claudia Cunningham, visit the grave of paranormal icon Charles Fort.

A few weeks later, a newspaper report declared that the "marauder" had been shot and was said to be a large black dog, which Cunningham claims was an early example of convenient "debunking," a pattern repeated throughout the history of the subject of demon dogs by the newspapers of the time. It appears that even in Fort's time, a media cover-up of the paranormal was firmly in place.

SWARTZ AND STEIGER STARE DOWN THE WEREWOLVES

Also included in *"Cryptid Creatures From Dark Domains"* is a chapter by paranormal researcher extraordinaire Tim Swartz, who writes about the folklore of his native Indiana. In the early 18th century, French fur trappers making their way south from Canada encountered their own version of the canine nightmare called the Loup-garou, a supernatural threat more frightening than any wild and predatory "earthly" wolf.

The Loup-garou often appeared as a monstrous wolf but could also shape-shift into a cow, horse or any other animal. The creatures were also said to have mental powers; under their spell, a human victim became an enraged animal that roamed at night through the fields and forests. During the day, the unfortunate reverted to his human form but was sickly and fearful to tell of his predicament. People at the time believed that such was the fate of those who violated the rules of the Catholic observance of Lent.

Swartz is also a scholar of cinema and provides several pages of background and poster art from movies about werewolves.

Not to be outdone, legendary paranormal writer Brad Steiger offers his chapter, called "The Terrible Hungers of Real-Life Vampires, Werewolves and Ghouls." The title alone should whet your appetite for Steiger's fascinating historical study of monstrous crimes committed before the advent of modern psychiatry, which taught us to attribute such things to simple human sadism and sexual perversion. In times past, Steiger writes, evil spirits got the blame, but perhaps we moderns should instead search "the wasteland of man's subconscious."

The reader will most likely agree that the new book covers the subject of supernatural canines very thoroughly, does it not? To which we can only add, "We double-dog dare you to take a walk on the wild side and read '*Cryptid Creatures From Dark Domains.*'"

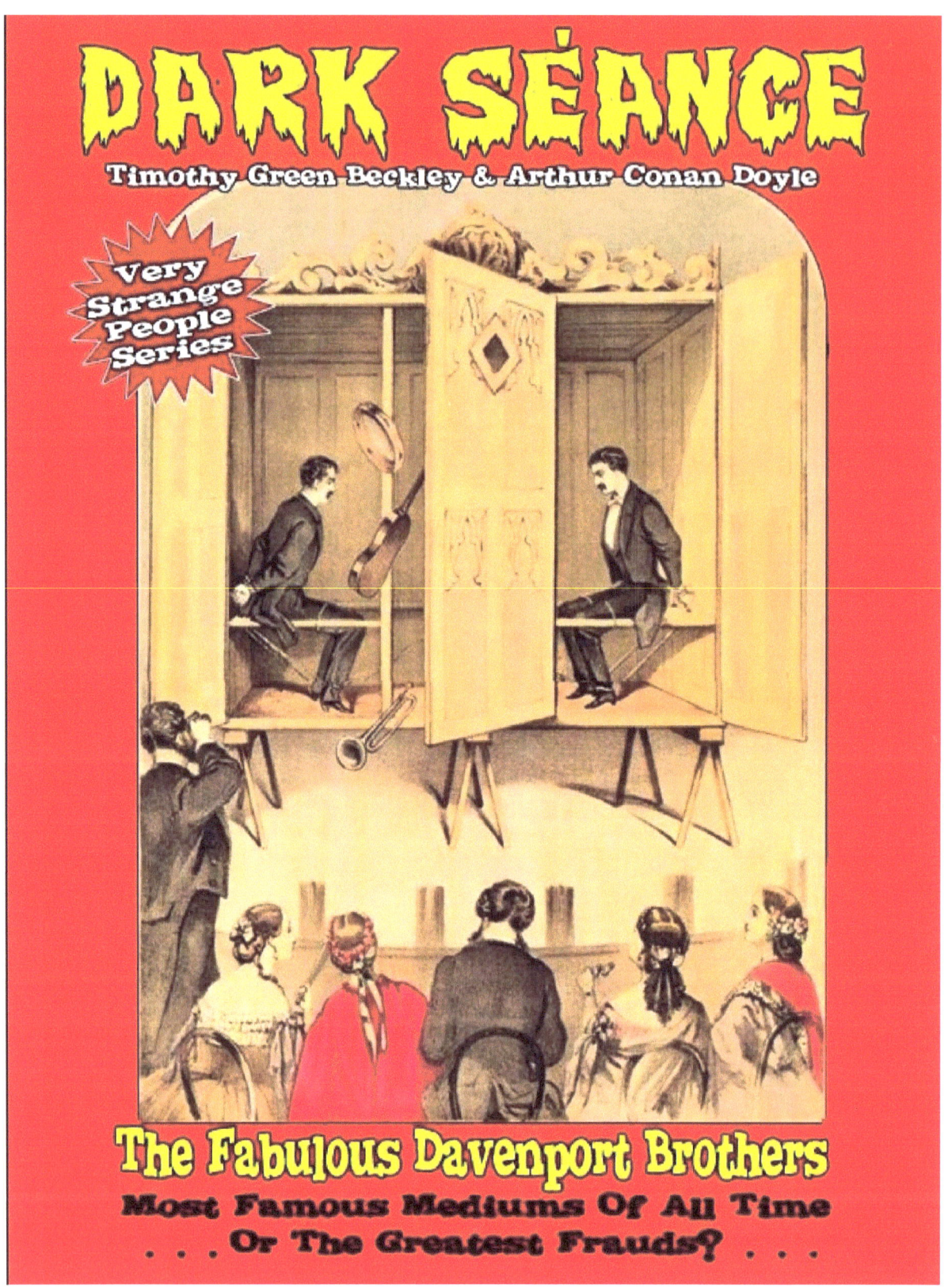

CHAPTER 11

UFOS, Mediumship and the Paranormal

By Sean Casteel

At one point in the history of America the belief in spiritualism was as strong – and as controversial – as the belief in UFOs is today. And a demonstrable parallel can be drawn between the two topics, which even seem to attract some of the same people across the various paranormal research fields – more so in recent years as increasing numbers come to accept the reality of UFOs as being at least partially of a paranormal or supernatural nature.

Spiritualism flourished beginning in the mid-19th century and for many decades held a fascinated general public in its thrall. Whether one was a believer or a determined skeptic, everyone had an opinion as to the reality of contacting the dead, with many others devoting their energies to the tireless debunking of fraudulent mediums who the skeptics thought were scamming the public and taking their hard earned money deceitfully.

What is Spiritualism? The most fundamental belief of the Spiritualists is that the soul survives physical death and that certain departed souls can communicate with the living. This communication is achieved through the agency of a medium, a man or woman who claims the distinct ability to speak with those who have passed away.

Mediumship traces its roots back to the ancient shamanistic traditions and is an extension of many priestly traditions as well. Most Native American tribes had at least one shaman or "medicine man" among them who would go into a specially prepared teepee and enter into a trance state (sometimes in a drug-induced state) in order to contact the ancestors of the tribe. Those standing outside the teepee could see mysterious shadows and figures moving about inside the lodge which could not have been the shaman. His hands were often bound and his posture secure – much like in a séance off the reservation.

A true medium can be a conduit for numerous Spiritualist phenomena, including prophecy (i.e., the Oracle of Delphi in ancient Greece). He or she may also be capable of clairvoyance and clairaudience, possess the gift of speaking in tongues and of healing by the laying on of hands. They may see visions and enter easily into a trance. A medium can also summon spirits and guides from the world of the dead and even cause the voices of the departed to speak aloud to a gathering of the living at a séance.

A distinguished British physicist and chemist, Sir William Crookes, around the turn of the 20th century categorized certain physical manifestations of spiritualistic activities. These include:

The Shaking Teepee Phenomenon is common throughout Native American culture. A shaman will enter a teepee and the shadows of spirits will appear even though the medicine man is bound so that he cannot move about.

*** The movement of heavy bodies with contact but without mechanical exertion.

*** The phenomena of percussive and other similar sounds.

*** Movements of heavy substances when at a distance from the medium.

*** The rising of tables and chairs off the ground, without contact with any person.

*** The levitation of human beings.

*** The movement of various small articles without contact with any person.

*** Luminous appearances.

*** The appearance of hands, either self-luminous or visible by ordinary light.

*** Direct (automatic) writing.

*** Phantom forms and faces.

*** There is also the possibility of special instances that seem to point to the agency of a superior intelligence as well as miscellaneous occurrences of a complex character.

All of which sounds like a motherlode of the strange and bizarre and calls to mind many of the claims made by UFO abductees. This relationship between Spiritualism and UFOlogy has often been noted by Timothy Green Beckley, the CEO of the publishing houses Global Communications and Inner Light Publications. While Beckley is widely known as Mr. UFO, he has also long been interested in spiritualistic and occult matters and has republished classic works in the field.

The latest such offering from Beckley is *"We Can Awaken the Dead: Evidence of an Afterlife Now!"* It consists mainly of the personal journey to Spiritualist truth made by Vice Admiral W. Usborne Moore, a British naval officer who publicly advocated the notion that we can communicate with our departed loved ones.

The most fundamental belief of the Spiritualists is that the soul survives physical death and that certain departed souls can communicate with the living.

MODERN SPIRITUALISM

Moore began as a skeptic. He talks of reading a book, at the recommendation of an acquaintance, by the aforementioned William Crookes called "Researches into the Phenomena of Modern Spiritualism," which Moore said had led many people to the subject. Readers marveled that Crookes' credentials as a scientist did not deter him from expounding at length on the existence of "forces exercised by invisible intelligences."

Moore decided to test the waters himself and went to visit a clairvoyant named Mrs. Crompton, in Portsmouth, England, in 1904.

"She clairvoyantly saw a spirit form near me," Moore writes, "that answered very nearly to 'Iola' as I remember her."

Another medium, a Mr. Vango, described Iola to Moore two or three times, giving her name.

Sir William Crookes photographed at a séance with the spirit known as Katie King.

"These were the first intimations I received," Moore explains, "of the desire of my relative to get in touch with me."

As time passed and Moore visited other mediums, Iola continued to reach out to Moore.

"To be brief," Moore writes, "I found that the deeper I went into the study of Spiritism, the more apparent it became that, whether he wished it or not, man's individuality was not extinguished at death. I read books, visited clairvoyants, and attended séances for materialization. Through all of this I was constantly reminded of the existence of a near and dear relative, older than myself, who passed away thirty-seven years ago in the prime of her life. Her continued reappearances could only lead me to one conclusion: I was being guided to a reconsideration of the problem of immortality.

"At last, I have come to the absolute conviction," he continues, "that what we call 'death' is a mere incident, a door to a higher life that is, in reality, more substantial to the senses we shall hereafter possess than the one we set so much store upon here. The near relative who had proved to me this valuable truth is called in this volume 'Iola,' a spirit name which she herself adopted to avoid the unpleasant complications that may arise as to her identity among those of her friends and relatives who are not educated in Spiritism."

Thus Moore was drawn to the subject by his lost relative reaching out to him and not the other way around. Iola seemed to reenter his life from the world of the dead completely unbidden and without prompting on Moore's part.

Along with his heartfelt belief in the genuineness of Spiritualism, Moore also took aim at the debunkers.

"Nothing they write has tallied with what I've seen," he declares. "For a concrete instance of the foolish suggestions put forward by these ignorant 'know-it-alls,' I would point to a recent work in which there is a description of how slate-writing is performed."

Slate-writing falls into the category of "physical" spiritualist phenomena in which a spirit takes chalk in hand and write messages from beyond on a small slate.

"The writer says the sitter brings his own double slate," Moore writes, "and the psychic deftly inserts a small piece of chalk previously prepared by being mixed with steel filings. While the slate is being held under the table or elsewhere, the psychic moves the chalk by means of a magnet concealed up his sleeve and does it as in mirror writing."

The debunking writer unequivocally says the deceiving medium's use of this method is unassailable fact, but Moore quite pointedly differs.

"This statement of 'fact' is untrue," Moore argues. "Such a thing cannot be done. Even with an electromagnet in open sight it would be impossible to write twenty legible words. With a man sitting near you and watching you it is not possible to write five legible words without detection."

Nevertheless, Moore admits, books by debunking authors sold well and perhaps helped the naysayers to climb the social ladder of the time.

"For the majority of educated people are anxious not to be disturbed in their amiable doctrines of a Day of Judgment," Moore reasons, "and a fiery material hell in store for those who do not agree with them."

Readers at this juncture will observe that the way the skeptics behaved during the heyday of spiritualism is similar to the debunkers today who go out of their way to discredit many UFO experiencers, be they abductees or the much more tainted contactees of the late 40s and 1950s.

Early on in his book, Moore describes other physical phenomena he had personally witnessed, which included the materialization of heads and busts of discarnate entities, spirit singing, whispers and the flight of a musical instrument around the room and over the heads of the sitters, all the while playing a definite tune.

"I saw and heard a number of things," Moore writes, "that could not be explained by any system of juggling or deception of any sort."

THE DAVENPORT BROTHERS – THE GREATEST PHYSICAL MEDIUMS OF ALL TIME?

Such physical manifestations as Moore described were an everyday occurrence for the Davenport Brothers, a duo of American spiritualists whose talents were celebrated by none other than Sir Arthur Conan Doyle, the creator of the immortal detective Sherlock Holmes. Doyle had manufactured a character whose skills as a logician solved many crimes, but Doyle himself was given to more mystical beliefs. His struggle against the magician and escape artist Harry Houdini over the veracity of Spiritualist claims – including that of the Davenports – is well-known. Beckley has published a book [see the Suggested Reading list at the end of this article] dealing with their very public conflict as well as other strange theories about Houdini's "hidden powers."

Beckley has also published *"Dark Séance: The Fabulous Davenport Brothers,"* which is in part a reprint of a detailed account of their careers written in the early part of the 20th century. Their story began in 1846, when the Davenport family was disturbed by what they described as "raps, thumps, loud noises, snaps, cracking noises, in the dead of night." Not knowing how to respond, they simply did nothing.

A few years later, when the famous Fox Sisters began making headlines for experiencing similar things, ten-year-old Elizabeth Davenport declared that if such things happened to anybody, they might as well happen to them. The Davenports gathered around their table, placed their hands upon it, as they had read the Fox Sisters had done, and waited to see what would happen. After a few moments a movement as of swelling or bulging was felt in the table, then crackling noises, tippings, raps, and, finally, very loud and violent noises.

Ira Davenport, five years older than his sister, Elizabeth, was "taken with a violent propensity to write, his hand becoming subject to extraordinary gyrations. These messages were believed to be quite beyond both his mental or physical powers, and contained matters known only to the persons to whom they were addressed, and quite beyond his personal knowledge."

The Davenport Brothers managed to produce all sorts of phenomena while they were chained in a special spirit cabinet. Musical instruments would play and fly around the room of their "own accord."

Ira Erastus Davenport and William Henry Davenport.

Another incident in this early stage of the Davenports' development involved the knives, forks and dishes on the breakfast table beginning "to dance around as if suddenly imbued with vitality. In a few moments the table began to move, tipping up sideways, balancing itself on one leg and finally rising clear from the floor, floating in the air without the least support and moving in such a way that it was wonderful that the dishes upon it did not slide off and come crashing upon the floor."

Meanwhile, Ira's younger brother, William, had begun to communicate with an entity who said he was not of this Earth. The entity warned them to procure a large table for the better accommodation of those who would be coming from far and near to see these wonders for themselves. The family began to hold regular séances during which the physical manifestations were repeated in front of witnesses. Loud raps were heard; the table answered questions; spectral forms were seen in the flash of a pistol; lights appeared in the upper parts of the room; and musical instruments floated in the air while being played upon above the heads of the company.

The spirits somehow communicated to the Davenports that Ira and William should take their show on the road. They began by touring in Maine and obligingly permitted debunkers to thoroughly examine their equipment and to bind the brothers hand and foot so that no sleight of hand could be perpetrated. In spite of these conditions, the brothers were nevertheless able to conjure mysterious arms and hands that would play musical instruments.

While appearing in Philadelphia, the brothers were met with "violent opposition" from "philosophers," religious bigots, other spiritualists and people spoiling for a fight in general. It required fifty policeman to keep order. In spite of this, the brothers still produced the most extraordinary manifestations even before hostile crowds.

They continued to amaze observers and moved on to tour England and Scotland, appearing not only in theaters but also in private homes. In exclusive drawing rooms in London, they performed before not the "ignorant or the credulous," but a select company that included some of the sharpest minds in England, none of whom could see any method of deception on the part of the Davenport Brothers.

A writer for a London newspaper, *The Morning Post*, who was present for one such private séance, reported – somewhat bewilderedly – that, "Possibly they may be [clever conjurers] or it is possible that some new physical force can be engendered at will to account for what appears on the face of it absolutely unaccountable. All that can be asserted is that the displays to which we have referred took place on the present occasion under conditions and circumstances that preclude the presumption of fraud. Here is a field for the investigation of the scientific world."

Beckley's "*Dark Séance: The Fabulous Davenport Brothers*" also includes his own musings on the brothers and Spiritualism in general, with particular attention given to the similarities between Spiritualism and UFOs. It is certainly true that both fields cry out for serious study by the scientific community, as The Morning Post writer urged in his account of the London séance.

This has been but a brief overview of "*Dark Séance*," but the book itself is rich in fascinating detail. Ira died in 1911 and his brother William died tragically young at age 36 in 1877. Whatever the secret to their apparent miraculous powers was, it has never been disclosed or discovered.

THIRTY YEARS AMONG THE DEAD

While one reads Vice Admiral W. Usborne Moore and the Davenport Brothers in large part because they deal with physical manifestations of Spiritualistic workings, there is also another avenue explored in a book from Inner Light/Global Communications called "*Thirty Years Among the Dead*," first published in 1924. The book is still available in older, more expensive editions, but Beckley's version is the only one that can truly be called "complete and unabridged."

"Thirty Years" is not, as the title may suggest to some, a dull account of hanging around a morgue somewhere. It offers instead a still vitally relevant approach to abnormal psychology that is based on the idea that extreme mental illness is caused – not by a harsh environment or muddled brain chemistry – but by the encroachment upon the innocent by the discarnate spirits of the evil dead.

You may already be thinking that therein lies the stuff of a great horror movie, but you will be intrigued to learn that "Thirty Years Among the Dead" is a factual, well-documented account of treating and actually curing the mentally ill by contacting the oppressing spirits within the sufferer and convincing those spirits to leave.

To carry out this form of therapeutic spiritualism, a physician named Dr. Carl A. Wickland worked alongside his wife, Anna, an accredited medium who voluntarily allowed herself to be temporarily possessed by these wicked spirits in order to better understand their tormented motivations. The Wicklands would then use this information to treat the victims who so grievously suffered under these destructive otherworldly influences. Along with the mediumistic coercion of spirits conducted by his wife, Dr. Wickland would administer low voltage electric shocks to the patient's neck and spine with a device called a "Wimhurst generator," a wand-like instrument that worked to "dislodge" the wicked spirit of the dead.

UFO research also has a variety of unexplained photos of a paranormal nature associated with it – such as the photo of Elizabeth Templeton taken on an isolated hilltop in the UK. When the family photos were developed, a strange "spaceman"-like image appeared that was not visible when the picture was taken.

In his introduction to the new edition, Beckley explains that the Wicklands felt they had absolute evidence that these demented spirits of the dead liked to hang around the living in order to continue their evil ways even from the afterlife. In essence, they would leech onto those who were prone to similar fits of debauchery or were well on their way to a life of unabated revelry and eventual damnation.

"The influence of these discarnate entities," Dr. Wickland writes, "is the cause of many of the inexplicable and obscure events of earth life and of a large part of the world's misery. A recognition of this fact accounts for a great portion of unbidden thoughts, emotions, strange forebodings, gloomy moods, irritabilities, unreasonable impulses, irrational outbursts of temper, uncontrollable infatuations, and countless other mental vagaries."

Dr. Wickland points out that "records of spirit obsession and possession extend from the remotest antiquity to modern times," including the Old and New

Testaments and the Homeric legends. The Wicklands' work stands as an example of the power of certain Spiritualist practices to heal deep psychological and emotional wounds, something science is still groping in the dark to accomplish through medication and simple talk therapy.

And while it is true that Spiritualism cannot today claim the many millions of followers and believers it had in the years between 1850 and the early decades of the 20th century, Timothy Green Beckley is part of the process of keeping the movement in front of the reading public and demonstrating its continued relevance to many fields of the occult sciences and to the pursuit of the truth underlying UFOs and alien abduction. Beckley's publishing efforts may one day help the world to arrive at a kind of paranormal "Theory of Everything" where all the mysteries fit in their proper places – to the enlightenment of us all.

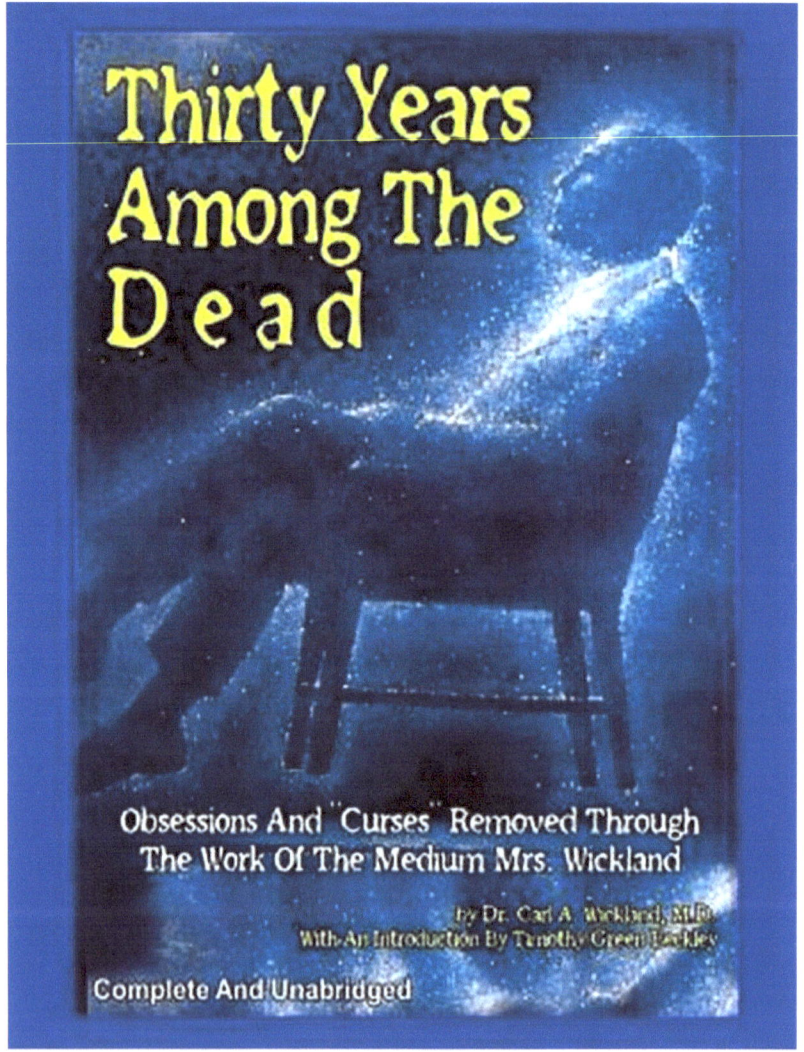

Thirty Years Among the Dead.

CHAPTER 12

Was Inventor Nikola Tesla a UFO Contactee?

By Sean Casteel

In the more than 70 years since his death, Nikola Tesla has never ceased to be a fascinating, mysterious figure dwelling somewhere outside the borders of history as it is understood by the unseeing masses. While we as a 21st century civilization continue to reap the benefits of his outsized genius, Tesla has yet to be given the recognition he deserves as a major architect of the relatively technologically comfortable age we live in.

Still, there are those of us who do give Tesla his due, belatedly but sincerely. This article will deal with an aspect of Tesla's genius that has gotten short shrift even from those of us who revere his name: UFO contact.

And that theory is nowhere better espoused than in *The Lost Journals of Nikola Tesla* by Tim R. Swartz. Swartz's bestselling classic has recently been updated and reissued by Global Communications and is worth a new look whether you've read the first edition or not.

I interviewed Tim Swartz a few years ago for one of Tim Beckley's now defunct newsstand magazines, and Swartz laid out some historical background of Tesla's earliest beginnings.

"Tesla was born in Yugoslavia," Swartz said, "in what is now Croatia, at midnight between July 9 and July 10 in 1856. He had that spark of genius right from the very beginning. There are a couple of people, I think, throughout our history, that you could classify as a 'super genius.' That's the best word I can think of. Most people would agree that Einstein was one of our greatest geniuses.

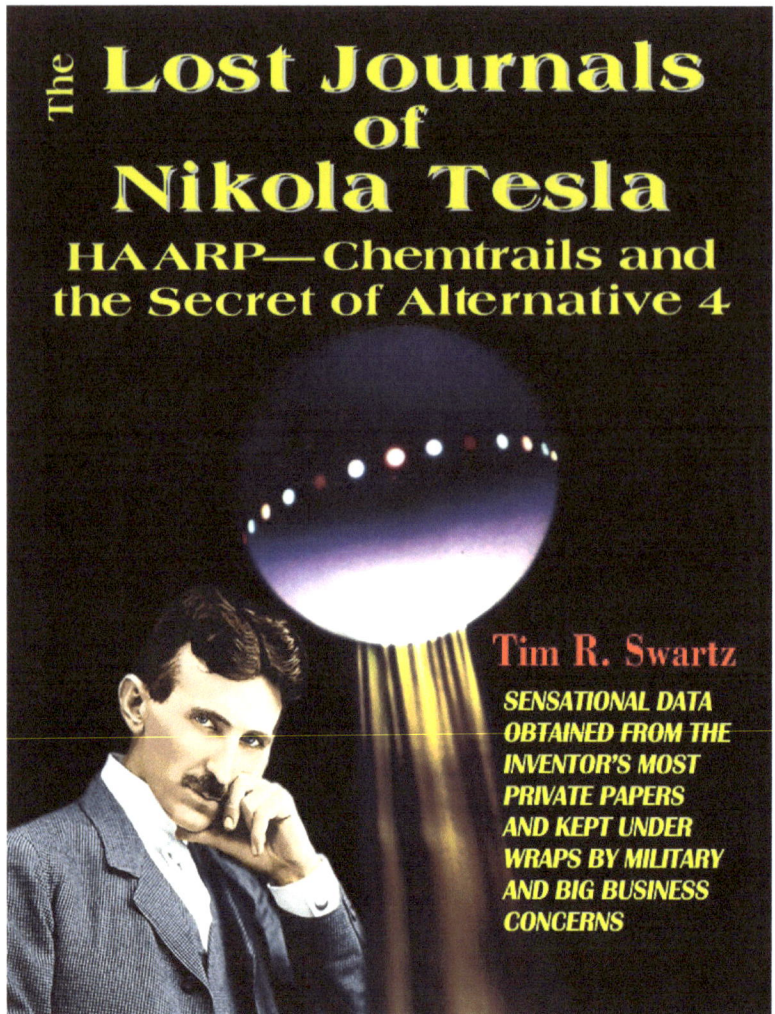

Maybe Leonardo da Vinci. And Nikola Tesla should fit right up there with those guys, because he just seemed to have this mind that was open to the universe.

"I suppose that's a rather esoteric way of looking at it," he continued, "but he had the ability to visualize his ideas to such a point that he could actually 'see' what he was visualizing in three dimensions. As he put it, 'It seemed to hang in the air right in front of my eyes.'"

Nowadays, Tesla is best known to the general public as the inventor of the AC motor.

"Our entire system of electricity," Swartz explained, "works with AC current. In Tesla's day, Thomas Edison had come up with a system to deliver electricity to houses and buildings based on the DC current, direct currents. DC current works fine, but it can't be sent over any great distance. Probably every half mile to a mile you would have to have a station that would step the power back up again and send it on for another half a mile or so. A very inefficient system and really only good for close areas like New York City. That's where Edison had initially done some wiring."

Tesla, by contrast, created a motor based on alternating current, which can travel hundreds of miles before it has to be retransmitted. This was a revolution for its time. Tesla came up with a working version of an AC motor and was the first to build, at Niagara Falls, a massive power generating station that supplied electricity to New York City.

"It was cheap, clean, efficient, and it actually worked," Swartz said. "That's probably Tesla's greatest claim to fame."

Tesla followed up that achievement by inventing radio. Though popularly credit for radio is given to Marconi, the Supreme Court declared some years after Tesla had died that Tesla's patented radio devices had preceded Marconi's and that Tesla is officially the father of radio. Tesla also created the first remote control device, which he demonstrated by directing a small battery-powered toy boat through various maneuvers on a lake as newspaper reporters looked on. He also designed a torpedo for use in warfare that was remotely controlled.

Tim R. Swartz

Tesla's laboratory at Colorado Springs, Colorado.

It was while working on a radio receiver designed to monitor thunderstorms that Tesla stumbled onto something quite extraordinary.

"Tesla thought that possibly he had received a radio signal from outer space," Swartz said, "that could conceivably be from extraterrestrials. Which is a pretty amazing concept for his time. Scientists back then were speculating that there could be life on Mars, but nobody suggested it too seriously. Tesla was conducting experiments in Colorado Springs, Colorado, in 1899, with a pretty good-sized radio receiver, because he was fascinated by the way lightning played in thunderstorms. He was trying to come up with a way to harness the power from thunderstorms.

"And one evening," Swartz continued, "he received what he called 'regular signals.' You know, like beep, beep, beep. Not the usual static you hear from thunderstorms and lightning. He wondered at the time if he wasn't listening to 'one planet greeting another,' as he put it. From that point on, it became somewhat of an obsession of his, to build better and better radio receivers to try to see if he could repeat what he heard. He got to the point where he claimed that he was actually receiving voice transmissions. He said it sounded just like people talking back and forth to each other. He made notes saying that he was actually hearing intelligent beings from another planet talking to each other, although he didn't know what language they were speaking. But he still felt he understood them."

An interesting point that should be made here is that at the time Tesla was hearing these alien voices through his primitive radio equipment, 1899, the country had just experienced the great Airship Wave of the late 1800s. No less a UFO expert than researcher and historian Dr. David Jacobs believes that is when true UFO contact first began, in the skies over America, when people familiar only with hot air balloons as real life flying devices began to see metal ships that flew over their homes and farmland, abducting the occasional cow and speaking to bewildered farmers in languages beyond their understanding. While one hesitates to abandon the more familiar Ancient Astronauts theory that says alien contact began with mankind's birth in prehistoric times, Jacobs' belief does tend to support what Tesla claims happened to him.

This also begs the question: Did aliens have some kind of part in leading Tesla to create what he did? It is argued in the controversial book *The Day After Roswell*," by the late Colonel Philip Corso and his collaborator Bill Birnes, that recovered alien technology was reverse-engineered and used to lay the groundwork for numerous inventions, including fiber optics and much else in the way of technology we take for granted today. One sometimes wonders if the aliens more likely are implanting the seeds for, or even directly "inspiring," through some process of implanted thoughts, some of the marvels of the current age.

In any case, there is likely some kind of overlap here between Tesla's voice contact and the inventions that came later, though it is of course impossible to prove. Tesla felt the voices were slowly preparing mankind for conquest and domination. In *"The Lost Journals of Nikola Tesla,"* Swartz goes on to recount the spine-tingling chronology of Tesla's battle with these aliens he believed to be an enemy race, all set against a background of industrial espionage and governmental secrecy that would make for a crackerjack science fiction tale were it not for the fact that the events are alleged to be completely real.

Tesla later went public with his claim that he was receiving extraterrestrial voice transmissions and was subjected to the usual humiliating ridicule that greets UFO witnesses today when they try to speak openly of their experiences. But he remained firm in his conviction that the voices were genuine and posed a terrifying threat to life on Earth as we know it.

Global Communications publisher Tim Beckley provided more input on the connection between Tesla and UFOs.

"There are many who believe," Beckley said, "that Tesla was actually a 'star child' of sorts, that he was born on another planet and left on the doorstep of his adoptive parents. This speculative theory was first offered in a long out-of-print book by Margaret Storm and a later book by our own Commander X titled 'Nikola Tesla: Free Energy and the White Dove.'

"The idea that Tesla was born off-planet," Beckley continued, "seems to have originated with a gentleman named Otis T. Carr. A Baltimore MD and inventor, Carr claims that he worked side-by-side with Tesla for years and that he discovered bits and pieces of the great inventor's life that no one else knew about, including the fact that Tesla wasn't originally from 'here.'"

According to Beckley, Carr later went on to invent a saucer-shaped device that he said for a mere $14 million would take us to Mars or somewhere else nearby in the solar system.

"Carr was a controversial figure in his own right," Beckley added, "but no one has been able to prove that he didn't work with Tesla in Manhattan, where Tesla was living in the New Yorker Hotel near Herald Square. We do know that Tesla was fascinated with the possibility of life on other planets."

Beckley reiterated Swartz's statements regarding Tesla's attempts to establish contact with the aliens via radio.

"And he might have been successful in reaching out to the stars," Beckley said. "Furthermore, Tesla is said to have even developed a 'Tesla Scope' that anyone could use to make contact with extraterrestrials. The device was on display in Canada for several years before its owner passed away."

Scale model of Otis T. Carr's OTC-X1 space ship.

Now a few words about the title of Swartz's book. Tesla died in 1943, in poverty and relative obscurity. As he moved from hotel to hotel, staying one step ahead of his debts, he often left behind whole suitcases full of notes and diagrams for unfinished inventions. Legend has it that after he died, the federal government stepped in and confiscated the material, believing it contained designs for new weapons devices and therefore was relevant to national security.

But apparently a few things slipped through the fingers of the government. At a 1976 auction in Newark, New Jersey, a collector named Dale Alfrey bought four boxes of papers for around $25. Alfrey at first thought he had purchased the notes of a science fiction writer and had no idea of the importance of what the boxes contained. Twenty years would pass before Alfrey began to actually read the material and to try to preserve the badly mildewing papers by scanning them into his computer. While he was absorbed in this effort, he was visited by a trio of Men-In-Black who looked to him like "undertakers." They offered to buy the papers from Alfrey, who replied that they weren't for sale.

After further discussion, which included some disturbing threats from the MIBs, the three visitors turned in unison and walked away. Alfrey felt himself to be regaining consciousness after being in a kind of trance. When he rushed back inside, the papers were gone, and so was the hard drive to his computer. He never completely recovered from the experience with the MIBs, but he did retain enough of what he had read of Tesla's lost journals to be sufficient for Swartz's book. Meanwhile, newspaper accounts from the time of Tesla's death related that a dozen large boxes of Tesla's notes may still be unaccounted for, perhaps waiting to be rediscovered and give up their secrets in our time.

This newly revised and expanded second edition of "*The Lost Journals of Nikola Tesla*" by Tim R. Swartz also contains new chapters on Time Travel, Alternative Energy, and Nazi flying discs, all of which help to expand the range and depth of the legacy Tesla has left to us to assist in our 21st century groping for technological mastery of our world. If we ever learn to travel in time or to take our energy directly from the forces animating the universe or even to slip the surly bonds of Earth in a disc-shaped craft of human design, our debt to Nikola Tesla can only increase.

CHAPTER 13

Diane Tessman - From UFO Investigator to Cosmic Citizen

By Sean Casteel

Diane Tessman has been in contact with "otherworldly entities" from her earliest childhood. While some people merely dabble in the study of ufology before moving on to some other temporary obsession, Diane has been immersed in the reality of the UFO phenomenon her entire life. She has written about her experiences extensively and has gathered a following eager to hear the messages from her spirit guide, a being named Tibus.

Timothy Green Beckley, the head honcho of the publishing company Inner Light/Global Communications, has recently published a greatly expanded version of Diane's first book, from 1983, with new material and updates, making it over 300 large format pages. The newly-renovated book is called "*The Real Life UFO Transformation of Diane Tessman: A Continuous Close Encounter with Future Man — Space Man.*"

What makes Diane's life journey so fascinating – and so different from others who have related their personal endeavors with the Ultra-terrestrials – is that she had made the full transition from UFO investigator for the influential MUFON and APRO groups to an abductee whose experiences have been verified (as much as scientifically possible) by several members of the academic community, to an individual who is actually able, she says, to communicate with her "Special One," a human-looking individual who she has come to believe represents "future human." Diane does not deny the possibility that some UFOs may come from outer space, other dimensions or parallel dimensions. "It's a big universe," she says, "and therefore I am open to a multitude of theories."

"Where do I begin?" Diane asks in her preface. "It was a long time ago that I wrote '*The Transformation*' on a $5.00 garage sale typewriter, which, in 1983, was considered a very old-fashioned typewriter. It was a heavy beast which weighed about a ton. I knew I had a lot to say. Much of it was not generated by my mind but catapulted into my head from outside. It was from an 'unknown,' but I somehow knew and loved that unknown."

It is most reassuring to read Diane's continual testimony about her contact with Tibus being rooted in love. The fact that she "knew and loved that unknown" extends beyond herself to the Planet Earth itself, which is in dire need of some form of intervention in order to survive. Diane writes that, in spite of the passage of many years since she wrote her first book, the message of her contact Tibus remains the same: he is part of an effort to love and protect Mother Earth and all her lifeforms and to guide humankind through this time of change and upheaval.

"Throughout the years," Diane writes, "he predicted what has come to pass with climate chaos and change, the tragic extinction of many species, social unrest, mass hysteria, mass insanity, and even deadly viruses which emanate from humans transgressing upon nature. However, Tibus had a great hope for our planet way back in 1983, just as he does today. "

AN EARLY AWAKENING

Diane had long had an ongoing relationship with the study of the nuts-and-bolts aspects of the UFO phenomenon, being a member of the Mutual UFO Network and the Aerial Phenomena Research Organization, but, in 1981, she decided to explore another aspect of UFO contact by undergoing hypnotic regression with well-known psychologist Dr. R. Leo Sprinkle. Under hypnosis, Diane recalled her earliest UFO encounter:

"I'm playing with Pat, my dog, on the farm. And I had stayed out late and Mom is inside cooking. Father's inside. I don't know where my brother is. The stars are clear. It is chilly, November. I am seven years old. And I have contact with something that has contacted me before, but I'm not allowed to remember. I want very much to remember them, though, and I try very hard. But this night I worry about Pat, my dog, when I go with them. They say he is all right.

"And there is someone onboard I know in particular, and I've known him each time. I'm not scared and I'm special, as other people are, but that to function in this life, in the mundane part of life that I have ahead of me, as protection, I cannot know the other side of me for a while, nor remember all that has happened. I love my mother and father, but every time I see them, I feel that this is where I belong. I always hate to leave. I always want to remember, but at that point it is not allowed."

Diane says the entities she sees onboard the craft look fairly much like humans.

"The one I know best is human," she says, "and I love him. There is something between us."

She calls the one she knows and loves her "Special One," and she will eventually come to call him "Tibus." It seems that Diane was never formally "introduced" to Tibus, but rather had known him all her life without any conscious recall of "how."

Diane has traveled the world to experience and commune with Gaia, the conscious spirit of Earth.

As part of this experience at age seven, Diane says "I know that I will be watched – or monitored – throughout my life, until the point comes where I finally enter the world where I belong, where they are. I'm reassured."

TIBUS SPEAKS

Tibus is quite the vocal presence in Diane's work. The Future Man Space Man of the new book's title, describes their relationship as "an experiment in shared consciousness between two individuals. Our sharing is a thing of joy and wonder to both of us, but we could not be sure at first that it would turn out as well as it has."

Tibus recalled that when Diane was typing out the original "*Transformation,*" she was sitting on the floor of her duplex apartment because she couldn't afford any furniture.

"I couldn't be sure," Tibus says, "that our shared consciousness would work, but, as the book progressed, I realized my messages were getting through loud and clear. I send them telepathically and they land in her head, often a few paragraphs long, then she hurries to write them down accurately."

There are some mind-bending aspects of time travel in the relationship.

"As individuals," Tibus says, "Diane and I have much in common. You might even wonder if she is me in a previous lifetime or I am her in a future lifetime. Ah, well, possibly so. She and I always proclaim that we are both separate, physical individuals, but we do acknowledge symbiosis, not only in working with our messages but as individual spirits as well.

"The difference is," he continues, "I am of the future from her point of view and yours. But all time is simultaneous! I have always promised that Earth and the human species do make it into the future. As a human from the future, I am proof of this. However, I realize that having a conduit of shared consciousness with Diane is not what most scientists call 'proof.' My coworkers on starships and time-ships are indeed extraterrestrials from far different planets, as well as humans of my (future) time. We do have the key to time travel, and you will soon also.

"The entire magnificent galaxy and the incredible universe beyond awaits humankind at The Moment – a moment of humankind's own choosing. Out there, that-a-way, is a magnificent quilt of multiple interdimensional worlds. But first mankind needs to make one small step up the awareness ladder. I speak of humankind as one collective consciousness.

"However, you have to CARE about the fate of Earth and her animals and CARE about your fellow humans. Be an activist in bringing our new world!"

MORE ON TIME TRAVEL

The predominate theme of "*The Real Life UFO Transformation of Diane Tessman*" grapples with the nature of time and the many different ways it is manifested and experienced. The new book includes an interview with Diane conducted by one of her fellow UFO researchers, who goes by the name Quantum Shaman.

Quantum Shaman asks Diane: Why are you so involved and even defensive of the concept that UFO occupants are time-traveling humans? I know you have faced a lot of criticism from people who hold fast that UFO occupants are aliens from far distant solar systems.

Diane: This is the first sentence of my book, "Future Humans and the UFOs," published in February 2020: "I do not deny that there are probably thousands of advanced extraterrestrial races in the galaxy and that some may visit Earth. However, I think we have ignored what is right before our eyes: our children's children's children are the occupants in most or all unidentified flying objects."

I am not excluding aliens from being among our strange visitors. I am merely trying to bring to light the fact that we have not seriously considered that time traveling humans are here also, in the flying vehicles that we will create in the relatively near future.

Quantum Shaman: What is your conclusion then about abductions? Do humans actually abduct other humans?

The human evolutionary line leads to humans in the future who look like what we think of as "extraterrestrials."

Diane: Of course they do! We abduct each other all the time. What else is kidnapping? We murder each other; we molest each other, "we" being our species. In our history, we have taken each other as slaves and we have committed genocide. Future humans may want to know more about the biology of their ancestors, either for scientific research or perhaps they need our DNA for some reason. Certainly most abductions do include tissue samples being taken.

Humans are a flawed, adolescent species. I do not claim that UFO occupants are angels. We can be cruel and self-serving. Isn't this how we current humans are too? We fail to consider that future humans visit us from all different levels of time. Of course, once we conquer time, we are perhaps timeless. However, there is no doubt that our species is behind in spiritual evolution while we excel at tech and science.

What will we be in 500,000 years, which is just a drop in the bucket of time? Will we have grown even more selfish? Or will we have evolved spiritually? Long story short, Tibus is not from 35 years ahead, but from hundreds or possibly thousands of years ahead. He is truly timeless in that he is a citizen of the cosmos as much as he is a citizen of Earth. He has learned the lesson, finally, that humans have taken so long to learn. And so, there is no contradiction between Tibus' spiritual messages and the future human premise.

Diane and Gabriel Green, George van Tassel's famous friend who ran for President of the U.S.

TIBUS HOLDS FORTH ON THE FLUID NATURE OF TIME

In one of the many messages from Tibus included in the book, he talks about transcending time altogether.

"Most people on Earth accept that time ticks along just as the river keeps flowing downstream and that this is an absolute that can never be overcome. However, with advanced technology and/or with a mind/soul of a higher frequency, one may head upstream just as if you had a motorboat to help you go against the current. Or, one may simply stand on the bank of the river and observe what was and what will be, as well as what is. Also, you must realize that there are other rivers (other timeframes, other dimensions/frequencies) flowing consecutively with the Earth river.

"We have stood on the bank of Earth's timeline/history since human life began on Earth. There are souls among us whose unique essence very much belongs to our frequency/dimension who volunteer to live on Earth for a lifetime, awaiting contact from us, for this promise from HOME never leaves their hearts and souls. In a sense, we infiltrate. Our star people are on lifetime 'espionage' missions. However, these missions are ones which are only to enlighten Earth, to gently guide her, to quietly raise the raise the frequency level, to pave the way for a higher dimension but within Earth's historical timeline.

"We do not overtly interfere or change history or meddle unless individual crises do not allow otherwise; and even then we often choose to allow the mundane dimension's karmic debts to be enacted, lived out, fulfilled – so that the higher dimension may occur naturally."

SCIENCE AND SPIRIT

For nearly four decades, Diane and Tibus have run a joint venture called "The Star Network" with which they reach out to fellow believers with a regularly published newsletter and monthly group meditations intended to help envision a new and better day for Mother Earth.

"Channelers usually give a message and then move on," Tibus writes, "never going back to be accountable for the information they offered. For perhaps the first time in the world of channeling, Diane and I are happy to offer input on our original messages where need be."

Which is a big part of why "*The Real Life UFO Transformation of Diane Tessman*" is such a valuable source of information. The new book not only revisits Diane's classic "The Transformation," it also adds a perspective from the future in which many of the messages are reevaluated or given the benefit of years of hindsight, an important factor in any endeavor that deals with the bending of the fabric of time.

"This book contains science and it contains spirit," Tibus says. "Reality is composed of both."

Diane can be contacted by email at: dianetessman0@gmail.com

Her mailing address is:

Diane Tessman

PO Box 352

Saint Ansgar, IA 50472.

www. EarthChangesPredictions.com

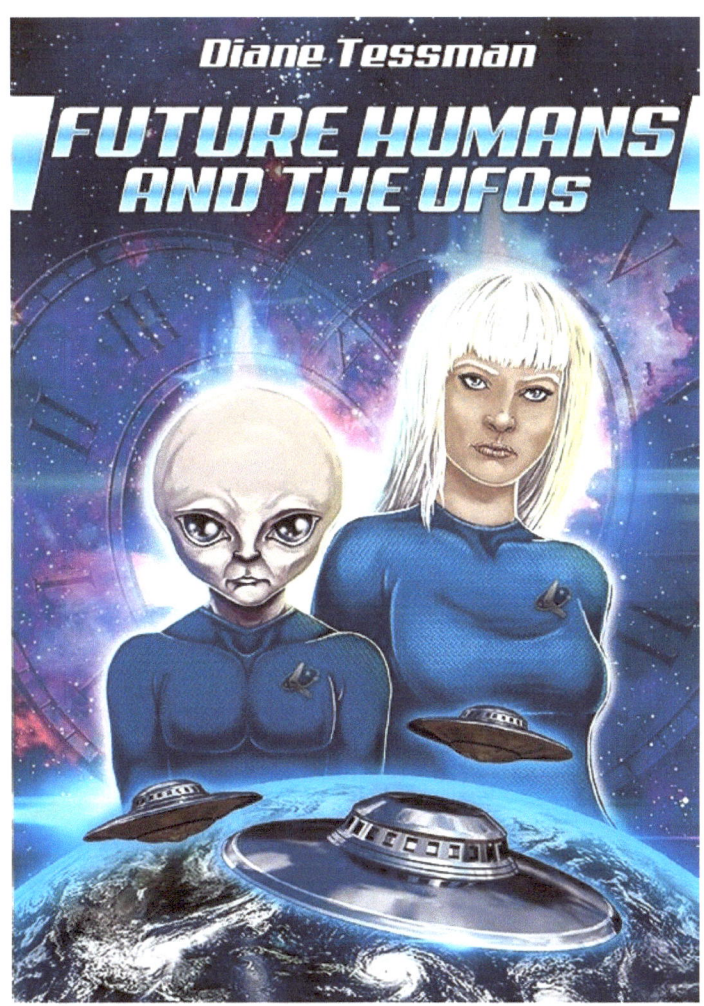

Diane Tessman's book "Future Humans and the UFOs." Published by Flying Disk Press.

"CONFESSIONS OF A TIME TRAVELING UFO GODDESS"

Many books have been written about UFOs. Some focus on sightings. Others on close encounters. Or even abduction experiences. Its rare to find one that includes all these categories, but also focuses on the life experience of the individual whose very existence has been drastically altered due to the dynamic nature of this phenomena.

The honey blonde, green eyed UFO experiencer underwent a series of face-to-face contacts with her "Special One" at an early age. This unique relationship resulted in a bonding between a cosmic and an earthly soul. Their relationship has lasted all of Diane's life leading to wisdom about the nature of the universe, include space and time travel.

Her work is a unique, inspiring, fun adventure which offers personal, never before documented, alien and paranormal experiences of a UFO abductee, channel, researcher, and world explorer.

You can order **"THE REAL LIFE UFO TRANSFORMATION OF DIANE TESSMAN"** directly from the publisher for only $20 (plus $5 shipping).

For PayPal Orders and more information: mrufo8@hotmail.com

CONTACT DIANE DIRECTLY FOR SPECIAL OFFERS – AND FIND OUT HOW SHE CAN HELP YOU...PAST LIFE READINGS, CHANNELING, PLUS SPECIAL CRYSTALS!

www.earthchangepredictions.com

DianeTessman0@gmail.com

Books are available as printed books or as Kindle ebooks at Amazon.com

Unsolved Mysteries! Hidden History! Unexplained Phenomena! Censored Events!

☐ **UFO REPEATERS—THE CAMERA DOESN'T LIE!— $24.00**

Here are the fantastic but true accounts of people from Turkey to New York City who claim repeated contact with Ultra-terrestrials. What makes their experiences so unique are the photos as evidence of their claims. Not blurry shots, but real hardware that came, they say, from space. Many have had numerous encounters, including Howard Menger, Marc Brinkerhoff, Ellen Crystal and Paul Villa.

☐ **2 BOOKS! — WHAT DOES THE BIBLE SAY ABOUT LIFE INSIDE THE EARTH? DOES ATLANTIS EXIST AT THE CORE OF THE PLANET? — $22.00**

Is There A Golden Paradise Inside Our Earth? Who Pilots The Ships We Call UFOs? Are They Here To Harm Or Help Us? Are the Residents Of This Subterranean World Angels or Devils? Atlantis is NOT a Water World! Why the ban on this information by the Church for centuries? Over 400 large size pages.

☐ **READ OTHERS THOUGHTS AND COMMAND THEIR THINKING! - $24.00**

Learn what others are thinking about you. Learn to command thought waves and mental whirlpools! Don't let others dominate your life. Learn to be strong!

☐ **2 BOOKS — FATIMA PROPHECIES AND SECRETS OF THE POPES — $22.00**

Has the "Secret 3rd Prediction" ever been fully revealed? Does it proclaim the End of Days? What secrets does the Vatican archives hold? Was one Pope really a woman? Is Satanism practiced in the Church? Want to know more? ☐ Add $15 for our hard hitting 90 minute DVD.

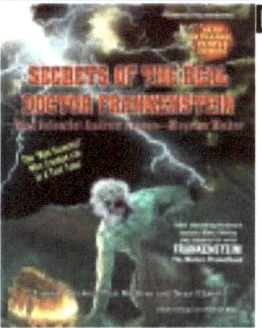

☐ **SECRETS OF THE REAL DOCTOR FRANKENSTEIN — $15.00**

The "Mad Scientist" who created life in the laboratory. Science said he was delusional and a fraud. But he did what others have not done since his death in 1855. His research inspired Mary Shelly's "Frankenstein" novel.

☐ **2 STUNNING BOOKS ON UFO CRASHES AND GOVT COVER UPS — $24.00**

What is hidden in the mysterious "Blue Room" At Wright Patterson AFB? Does MJ 12 exist? Is Disclosure coming? # 1 — "The Case For UFO Crashes," and #2— Frank Scully's "Behind The Flying Saucers," the examination of a spaceship retrieval. ☐ Add $5 for audio lecture by scientist.

☐ **SPECIAL PAIR OF OCCULT BOOKS — $22.00**

Obtain riches in life and hold on to them after "you are gone!" Rev. Ike and Maria D Andrea explain how to take life's riches with you and how to obtain them now! — #1 "You Can Take It With You." —# 2 "Heaven Sent Money Spells." Free DVD workshop with Maria D'Andrea.

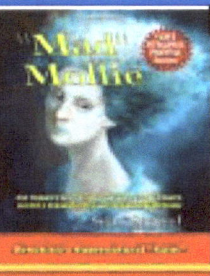

☐ **3 BOOKS "THE VERY STRANGE PEOPLE SERIES" — $39.00**

1 — "Matrix Control System of Philip K. Dick and the Paranormal Synchronicities of Tim Beckley.

#2 — "Mad Mollie — the Supernatural Enigma of Brooklyn," who didn't eat or sleep for 50 years.

#3 — "Davenport Brothers' Dark Seance," world's best physical mediums. 600+ pages.

☐ **HIDDEN SECRETS OF THE KNIGHTS TEMPLAR, OAK ISLAND AND MASONIC ORDER — $18.00**

Today, we speak in terms of the Rockefeller Dynasty, the Rothschild banking family, Goldman Sachs, the Clinton Foundation . . . but, even if you merged all the vast wealth of these and many more conglomerates, you would get nowhere near the vast fortune of the Knights Templars which is buried closer than you think!

SPECIAL — ALL BOOKS THIS AD JUST $189.00 + $15.00 S/H • Add $$ for extra items like DVDs, etc.

WE ACCEPT CHECKS, MONEY ORDERS AND PAYPAL

Explore These Way Out Worlds!

HOT NEW TITLE JUST RELEASED!

HAVE UFO MASTERS ESTABLISHED BASES IN YOUR NEIGHBORHOOD?
ALIEN STRONGHOLDS ON EARTH — $20.00

There is evidence that human-looking ETs are living down the road, hidden in some secluded base of operations. They have been seen to emerge from a landed craft and then observed in the checkout line of the local supermarket. Should they be "found out" and followed into the parking lot just a few feet away, they are seen to vanish right before the eyes of stunned witnesses.

Some UFO strongholds are believed to be located high in the mountains – such as Mount Shasta, Mount Olympus, at the highest points of the Andes and around the red rocks of Sedona, Arizona. Other ET bases are located way back in the jungles of Mexico and

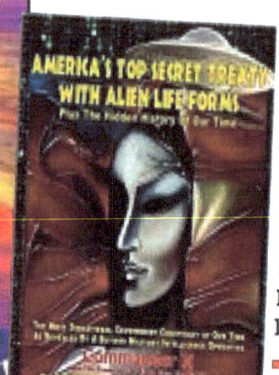

along the Amazon. Still others require diving and sonar equipment to pinpoint the aliens' watery world. Additional bases are "hidden" in plain sight. They could be in what seem to be abandoned buildings. Or out-of-the-way castles or mansions that can house a sizable encampment of Ultra-terrestrials. They might be concealed along darkened trails that lead to the swamplands of America, or in the underpopulated areas of Australia's Outback. One of the most hidden alien bases is believed to be within forty miles of the White House. You are invited to join our quest for the emerging truth about such potentially catastrophic cosmic matters. Who knows? Perhaps the next alien stronghold to be discovered might be just a few blocks away or down the road, right in your very own neighborhood. The Ultra-terrestrials' footholds on our earthly plane are numerous, and this book offers a unique look into some of these alien fortresses. *Includes material by* Timothy Beckley, Sean Casteel, Joshua Shapiro, Nigel Watson, Scott Corrales, Tim R. Swartz.. 270 pages, Large format - Many photos.

BIG BOOK OF INCREDIBLE ALIEN ENCOUNTERS
500 page, large format, guide to space aliens, interdimensional beings and Ultra-terrestrials. Witnesses have been harassed, fought with, paralyzed, abducted and sexually molested. Tim Swartz leads 25 researchers in search of the truth. $22.00.
ISBN 9781606119815

BIBLICAL UFO REVELATIONS
Dr. Barry Downing (long time MUFON contributor) asks: "Did Jesus leave earth in a spaceship? Did angelic beings part the Red Sea? Did "spacemen" guide Israelites out of the wilderness? What was manna? Ark of the Covenant? Ancient Astronauts in religious context. 200 pages, large format. $19.00.
ISBN 9781606112465

DEJA VU — UFOS OVER AND OVER AGAIN
Shapeshifters, skin walkers. Dozens of UFO hotspots. Stargates to distant realms and dimensions where you can skywatch. Morphing objects near enough to touch! 382 pages, large format. $21.00.
ISBN 9781606119893

THE REAL LIFE UFO TRANSFORMATION OF DIANE TESSMAN
Former MUFON/APRO investigator reveals continuous close encounters with a future man-spaceman. Bonding of an earthly and cosmic soul. Verified by Dr. Leo Sprinkle! Her experiences are UNEARTHLY! 315 pages, large format. $20.00.
ISBN 9781606119488

Order At: Amazon.Com (search title or ISBN). Or direct from the publisher
TIMOTHY G BECKLEY, 11 EAST 30TH STREET, 4R, NY NY 10016

MUFON SPECIAL: All 4 titles just $59.95 + $10 S/H. Send email mrufo8@hotmail.com for PayPal Invoice. Or credit card invoice. 646 331-6777, leaving all info and we will call back asap if necessary!

Subscribe To Our YouTube Channel —"Mr UFOs Secret Files." Over 400 interviews. KCORradio.com Thursday's at 10 PM Eastern for LIVE show.

FREE CATALOG - OVER 350 TITLES. DOZENS OF BEST SELLING AUTHORS.

www.ingramcontent.com/pod-product-compliance
Lightning Source LLC
Chambersburg PA
CBHW041528220426
43671CB00002B/20